Devil's
Dropout

CHRISTIAN PUBLICATIONS INC,
1230 - 17th AVENUE S.W,
CALGARY, ALTA.   T2T 0B8

Devil's Dropout

Manson follower turns to Christ

by Onjya Sipe
with Robert L. McGrath

mott media
P.O. BOX 236 MILFORD, MICHIGAN 48042

COPYRIGHT © 1976 by Onjya Sipe and Robert L. McGrath

LIBRARY OF CONGRESS CATALOGING IN PUBLICATION DATA

Sipe, Onjya, 1951 -
    Devil's Dropout.

    1. Sipe, Onjya, 1951 - 2. Conversion. I. McGrath, Robert L., joint
author. II. Title.

BV4935.S56A33   248'.2'0924 [B]   76-17648

ISBN 0-915134-16-0
ISBN 0-915134-17-9 pbk.

DEDICATED TO
Shemyiah . . .
with my earnest prayer
that she will some day
understand . . . and
know Jesus Christ as I do;
and
to my mother . . .
even though I hurt her
in so many ways,
I am thankful to God that
her mother-love has not
wavered, that our often-traumatic
relationship has brought us
closer together.

CONTENTS

PREFACE

My life-story in these pages has been set down for one specific purpose . . . a purpose you'll find revealed in the last chapter of the book.

Why "Devil's Dropout"? There's a double meaning: I deliberately dropped out of school, out of normal society, and then without realizing it, into the diabolic clutches of the devil. Later, praise God, I dropped out of Satan's bondage, to find the glorious freedom of life in Christ.

My association with the notorious "Manson Family" — the result of my misguided quest for the true meaning of life — is not something to look back on with pride, but if my purpose is achieved through publication of this book, thanks be to God!

Onjya Sipe
April, 1976

Any reader requests, comments, or inquiries for personal appearances should be directed to:

Onjya Sipe
c/o Christian Chapel
1920 S. Brea Canyon Cut-off
Walnut, California 91789

Devil's
Dropout

1

Get Lost, Death — I'm Not Ready!

With shaking fingers, I tried to bring the wavering match to the end of the cigarette. It wasn't easy. For one thing, I couldn't get my eyes to focus properly. They just didn't want to work. For another, my hand was trembling so much, I had no confidence at all that I'd be able to bring it off this time. This was the third match I'd used, just trying to light that one cigarette.

Unexpectedly, the smoke swirled into my mouth. I'd made it; I drew in heavily, then wished I hadn't. It tasted lousy — so what else was new? Wasn't everything lousy? Everything I did, everything I touched, everything. So why should my tenth cigarette in two hours be different? Impulsively, I squashed the smoke in the already over-full ash tray. Something had to give. And quick!

I reached for another cigarette, then pulled my hand back. I stood up — anything to change this unearthly pressure around me. But pain knifed across the right side of my lower back like an electric shock, reminding me again of the fist-sized lump sticking out from the kidney infection. I pulled up my tattered blouse and twisted my aching head to look at the yellowish skin, crowned with the fiery red of the infected area. Again I had that paralyzing thought: "Something's got to give!"

I could pop another pill — except that I'd taken the last of the bennies the night before, taken it with a special little ceremony of my own: "This is it, Onjya *(OHN-yuh)*. The last one. Face it! You've got to put down. It's the end of the line." I laughed to myself, and laughing was a bitter taste in my mouth. "What is it they say — speed kills? If they only knew!"

I knew, all right. I'd stayed high on speed for — how long had it

been? I didn't know. I didn't want to know. I only knew I wanted
the sinister visitor lurking outside the door of that dingy apartment
to get lost. I knew him, all right. I'd crossed his path more than
once. I'd even invited him in a few times. But now, knowing he
was there — waiting...waiting...waiting — I wasn't ready for him.
Get lost, Death!

The searing pain raked its dagger across my back again, and in
desperation, I sat down and reached for another cigarette. Anything to take my mind off the miserable failure I'd become. I
looked through the twitching orange flare of the match at Erutan
(air-OO-tuhn), stretched in typical grassed-out haze on the sagging
divan across the room. No point in turning to him for help. He'd
probably toss himself an acid-pot-wine bust for a week or more if I
opened the door and invited my villainous visitor in. Erutan,
whom I'd first known as Chuck, wouldn't mind seeing me dead.
He hadn't exactly turned into a model husband. But then, what
about me? Was I a wife anyone could be proud of? Not so it
showed.

Put down, Onjya! Put down! Well, I was, wasn't I? I'd taken
the last of the speed pills, the last bennie, the night before. Wasn't
I putting down?

Get lost, Death — I'm not ready yet! But what to do? There had
to be some way. Of course, why hadn't I thought of it sooner? Call
Paul! My younger brother, Paul Myers, the one person I'd been
able to depend on from as far back as I could remember. Call Paul.

The telephone wanted to dance beneath my uncertain fingers,
but with a surge of will, I made it stand still long enough to dial the
number. *Please, Paul, be the one who answers. I can't stand
talking to anyone else!*

"Hello?" A strong, confident voice for an eighteen-year-old guy.
The voice I wanted to hear, the voice I needed.

"Paul?" My own sound a mere squeak. "Paul, this is Onjya."
Then, remembering that he preferred the name I'd grown up with,
"JoJo."

"What's with you?" he said. "You sound — weak."

I tried to smile, thinking about this always-dependable brother
at the other end of the telephone line. "I — am," I agreed. "Paul,
can you come? Take me to the hospital? I'm..."

"Did you overdose?" Concern filled his tones. Paul knew my

habit, though we never talked about it because he was straight. "What is it, Joey?"

"P-p-putting down!" I managed to stutter. "And I've got a bad kidney infection, Paul. I — can't make it!"

"I'll be right over!" my brother said then. "You're at the apartment?"

Tears suddenly trickled down my cheeks. "Hurry, Paul!" I mumbled.

And then there was nothing to do but wait. Still jittery, I finally lit the cigarette, and through the smoke I could see bleary sketches of what had brought me to this unwelcome here and now that was all around me. I felt better, knowing help was on the way. I could sense that the disagreeable tenant of the hallway outside my door had edged further away, but I knew he hadn't disappeared. He was still around, hoping. *Get lost, Death. It isn't your turn yet!*

Waiting, I continued to glance backward over the twenty-one years of yesterdays that were my mixed-up life. Somewhere along the way, I'd taken a wrong turn — or two or three. I suppose it had all begun that October day in 1951 when my mother brought me home from the hospital and my three-year-old stepsister, Jeannette, walked over to see me for the first time. My mother set the pattern for our later lives: "What's the matter with you? Are you jealous of her?" Jeannette had done nothing to bring on the remark, but from that moment, she had less than no use for me. I'd been told all about it many times.

Then came the total absence of discipline in our home and a lack of love that lay suspended beneath our lives, only to surface from time to time in temper explosions that made for a miserable existence. Or perhaps my here and now was an obvious outgrowth of the thorny pathway I chose from the age of thirteen, when I first got busted for getting stoned on vodka at a guzzling party.

I got up and slowly crossed the room, ignoring the thrust of torment the swollen kidney splayed through me. In the bathroom mirror, I hesitantly faced what I was: an acne-scarred apparition with darkly-sunken eyes, hollowed jaws from long-departed molars, jaundiced skin stretched over weary bones, dirty-blond hair that strung unevenly toward a wasted torso. At twenty-one, I was an ancient crone. Was it really worthwhile for Paul to come to my rescue? I wondered.

Turning away in disgust, I looked at the one who had been, successively, my lover...my guru...my husband...my daughter's father...my downfall. No, that wasn't fair. I'd been my own downfall; though Erutan had contributed — mightily — I could not in fairness blame it on him. We had made our miserable bed together, and we had lain in it. Now we were no longer man and wife because Chuck (Erutan) Sipe had lain in too many other beds as well, and I was through with him. But at the moment, he couldn't have cared less. As so many times before, he was freaked out on grass — stoned to a glazed state on the marijuana that had long been his very lifeblood.

For me, it had been an endless quest, looking for the truth, whatever that was. I thought about it now. I'd hunted, fruitlessly, for all those twenty-one years. It was a 'search for a me' and it had met no success, for I still knew nothing of what life was all about. There was Buddhism...Hare Krishna...the Universal Life Church. I'd tried them all, but I was as confused as ever. Could there be yet another spiritual answer I had not tried?

Was I doomed to be a dope peddler, like Erutan Sipe, forever? We'd existed — a wretched existence to be sure — on that thin thread of togetherness most of our five years of union. And what about my daughter — our daughter, to be technically accurate — although Erutan had never taken interest in her. Could I ever claim her again? Would the good and great things I'd envisioned for Shemyiah *(she-my-ah)* Nyomi Sipe ever come about? Not with that scythe-bearing spectre waiting in the wings. *Get lost, Death!*

The word, the thought, flared other memories into my disarrayed consciousness. What about *the Family* — that unpredictable, indeed, unfathomable — group of misled, mixed-up robots under the diabolic domination of Charles Manson, who claimed to be Jesus Christ and in the same breath, Satan himself. Had I really plunged myself into the unprogrammed nothingness that was Manson's philosophy? I shivered. That strange cave-existence when we were caring for the Family-produced offspring — was it all some LSD-born hallucination, like I'd experienced on the many acid-trips I'd taken? The torpedo in my lower back stabbed at me again. Real enough, all right. The cave-life had been real enough, too. Just as Shemyiah's disappearance had been. Would I ever have my baby as my own again? *Hurry, Paul!*

I glanced once more at my husband — Chuck Erutan Sipe who, not long before, had said, "It's only fair, man. It's your turn to bring in the bread. It's lots easier for you." He actually thought he was doing me a favor! "So take the job in that topless bar, down on Alvarado Street. You ought to be able to turn over some pretty good cash on the side. I'll help set them up for you. Two or three beds a night, say at twenty-five bucks apiece, and you can bring in some good bread, man, real good!"

God in heaven — or wherever! How did it all happen? How could it have happened? What was the answer to it all? Was it too late? Was that ghostly shadow outside my door going to stalk in to wrap me into his shroud of darkness, after all? I shuddered.

"Paul!" I murmured, steeling myself against the piercing pain that swept me. "Please hurry — before it's too late!"

2

Early Years —
Fear, Frustration

From my earliest memories, nine words seemed to dominate my life pattern: "I want what I want when I want it!"

Looking back, I can only wonder how my poor parents coped as well as they did with a headstrong daughter who much of the time gave them only problems, with those problems getting heavier as the years went by.

They lived in East Los Angeles when I was born. My mother had been previously married and divorced, and already had a three-year-old daughter, Jeanette. Dad was a truck driver, working a regular eight-hour day, so that we could have had a normal, happy home life. Unfortunately, we didn't, except on rare occasions. What love there was remained unexpressed.

It was only in much later years that I realized life at home was different for us from what it could have been. The constant bickering between Mom and Dad, sometimes leading to actual physical clashes, is one of my most vivid recollections. And the bickering did not change with the passing of the years. Yet, who is to say that my own misbehavior in those years of growing up didn't provide a major cause for my parents' discord? Certainly I have no wish to point an accusing finger at Mom and Dad in the pages of this narrative. Rather, I want to tell it like it was, readily admitting I cannot determine the "why" of what developed in my life. I can only report the "how" of it.

When I was three, my brother Paul arrived, and from the beginning, we were always close. Not so with Jeannette as I was the "kid sister." I wanted to pal around with her, but she'd have none of it, chasing me away when she was with her own friends.

Again, I have no desire to blame Jeannette for what my life became, for if she had any part in it, I'm sure it was minor. But I did share closely with my younger brother both the joys and the disappointments of growing up. He was my kind; we always understood each other until I went my own willful way while he, perhaps as a reaction to my own direction, stayed on an opposite, wholesome path. In our early years, I was one with him. I felt like he was me and I was him; we were that close.

My affection for my brother was probably a principal cause for one of the childhood incidents that may have helped shape my life. "JoJo, I don't want you playing with the water. You leave that garden hose alone!" My mother's words were as firm as they ever were. But all they did to me was to suggest a way I could get more attention. If I *did* play with the water, I'd be the center of family interest. I'd do it!

So I took the forbidden garden hose and began spraying the driveway; after all, this was something useful, I reasoned. Why should anyone fuss at me for that? I expect I may have been subconsciously doing something I thought Dad would approve, creating another source of conflict between him and Mom.

What I hadn't counted on was Paul running across the driveway, sliding on the slippery surface, and banging his head on the concrete. It opened a fair-sized cut, and the blood started streaming out.

I had no choice. "Mom!" I shouted, "Paul's hurt his head!"

By that time, Paul's own screams had attracted her, and I followed as she picked him up and scurried to the bathtub where she washed the wound to stem the bleeding.

I stood by, contrite and suffering for what I knew had been my fault. Our neighbor, Sarah, had heard the commotion and rushed over.

"What happened?" she asked anxiously.

Mom looked up from her ministrations. "JoAnn made Paul fall down!" she said, using the given name I had always hated. "Look at that cut!" And then to me, "You get out of here. You've done enough damage already!"

Dry-eyed, I shuffled away on dawdling feet. The last thing I'd wanted to do was hurt my brother, and like Mom said, I'd made him fall. In spite of the fear generated by my mother's chasing me away, I didn't go far. Minutes later, I stuck my head back into the bathroom where Sarah was helping Mom put a bandage over the gash.

"Is he — going to die?" I asked hesitantly.

"I told you to get out of here!" came the reply, ignoring my question. "Now go!"

Her command confirmed my suspicions: Paul had, indeed, suffered a mortal blow. I'd destroyed the best friend, the only brother I had. I trudged down the hall and looked out the front window to see that the hose was still running, water spilling over the driveway in a torrent of wastefulness. But I made no move to shut it off. My world was shattered. I would now be totally rejected by everyone around me; I knew it!

I have no idea how long the tremendous load of guilt I carried from that incident burdened me. I do recall that despite the fact that Paul's injury turned out to be only superficial, I worried about what had happened for many weeks. The only one who didn't voice concern — and contempt for me for my criminal negligence — was Dad. He had long since told Mom, with respect to raising us kids, "I'll just stay out of it." And for the most part, he did.

In fact, to the best of my memory, there was only one time when Dad lifted his hand — literally — to me. Paul and I had gotten into some sort of trouble, and he took a fly swatter to us both. It was the only spanking I ever got in my life, and I remember thinking how really mean Dad was for doing that. Perhaps if I'd been thoroughly spanked a good many more times...but it didn't happen.

From the age of four, I had a compulsion to steal things. It started simply enough; I used to go behind the fence to the neighbors' garbage cans. I'd go through them to find what I thought were things of value. Frequently, there would be worn-out, discarded toys, and I'd claim them for my own. Since my parents didn't notice, I began to feel I could gain from others even greater riches, so I began snitching jewelry from Sarah's house, next door. Down deep, I knew it was wrong, and I wasn't excited about the thrill of getting away with something. It was simply that I wanted the bracelet or the necklace or the earrings for my own, so I took them.

I remember getting caught once with a bracelet Mom

recognized as belonging to Sarah, but apparently she didn't think of it as any big go-round. "That's strange," she said. "That's really funny that you'd do that. Here, give it to me; I'll take it back to Sarah tomorrow."

No crime, no punishment. Just funny that I'd do it. If someone had bothered to sort out wrong from right, maybe things would've turned out differently. Mom was not entirely without effort in that direction. She did take us to church now and then. I think it was a Presbyterian Church, within walking distance of our East Los Angeles home. I recall getting interested in the arts and crafts activities of the Sunday school, but since we didn't go on a regular basis, church was relatively meaningless in my life.

What did have meaning was the kindergarten I started attending when I was five. Like many children, I didn't want to go that first day, and out of desperation, my baffled mother stuck me in Paul's baby stroller and wheeled me off to school. And more than once after that, she had to resort to the same tactics. On many occasions, I'd talk her into letting me stay home. Stuck with having to make all the decisions concerning her three children, she often just gave up, although I expect I was by far the worst in causing her headaches. From the very start, it appears, I held dominion over my mother — again good reason why I feel I must assume all responsibility for what my life became, rather than blaming her.

In any event, I finally began to discover that school wasn't all that bad, especially since it gave me the chance to work with paints, coloring books, and other materials I didn't have at home. And there were frequent festive times like Halloween, Thanksgiving, Christmas, and Easter to add special interest to the regular routine.

Take the incident when I thought my life was permanently splintered into tiny bits of nothing at Easter-time. My kindergarten teacher had given me the awesome responsibility of bringing a dozen colored eggs to school for our celebration, and I was really proud of the deep colors and unusual patterns I'd managed to create on the eggshells. I was anxious to get to school that day — so anxious that after I'd carefully cradled my beautiful eggs in a small basket, I hurried out the front door, caught my foot on the step, and sprawled headlong on the sidewalk!

The eggs went flying. As I hesitantly picked myself up off the walk, trying to pinch back impatient tears, I heard Mom's voice.

"JoJo Myers, can't you do anything right?"

I didn't answer. I picked up my first shattered egg and put it back in my now-empty basket. I hadn't intended to stumble on that step. At that particular moment, my gold-mine of Easter eggs had been the most important thing in the world to me. I was devastated!

"Well, hurry and get them picked up!" were Mom's next words. I didn't see any point in hurrying. Each egg I touched crumpled in my hand, its once-smooth surface now crinkled in a patchwork of broken dreams. I didn't want to go to school now, but for once, Mom was firm.

"You march right out that door and don't you look back!" she cautioned. "You messed up your eggs yourself, and you'll just have to make the best of it!"

I'd had enough Sunday school training at that point to know there was a heaven and a hell, and as I dragged my unwilling feet toward the kindergarten class that day, I was sure of only one thing: I was going straight to hell! I'd blown the most important assignment ever given to me — to bring a dozen Easter eggs to school. I thought of several alternatives; I could run away and never come back. But at five years old, I didn't really know how to do that. I could hide the eggs, and lie to the teacher, telling her my mother wouldn't let me bring any. But I wasn't sure I could get away with that one, either. I could tell the teacher a monster jumped on me on the way and broke all the eggs. But I wasn't sure I could explain what kind of monster it was, making me afraid of that alibi, too.

So I ended up hesitantly handing over my basket of crushed eggs to the teacher with a tearful three-word explanation: "I fell down!" I expected the sky to fall down on me, right then and there.

But that teacher was cool. "Well, now, JoAnn, don't you worry about that for a minute!" she said, patting my shoulder. "We have to crack the eggs before we eat them anyway, and yours are just a little bit ahead of the rest. Here — we'll just put them in a special place, so they'll be ready." She took the basket from my quivering hand. "And aren't they lovely!" she added, smiling at me.

Being blessed instead of blamed really blew my mind. My failure, my entry through the gates of hell, had turned into triumph. For the rest of that year, I did my level best to please my kindergarten teacher. It was one of the good times of my early life.

All too frequently, my school experiences were on the unpleasant side. From kindergarten on, there were many times when I stubbornly refused to go to school, and depending on Mom's mood of the moment, I was either allowed to stay at home, or else I was dragged — usually screaming — to my classes. By the time I was in the fourth grade, Mom had lost all control over me, and with Dad sitting on the sidelines as he'd previously declared, there was more than once when my uncle took over by force and saw that I went, practically dragging me into his car. And patterning my behavior on what I saw and heard at home, I could throw some pretty wild screaming tantrums.

There was the time when I walked into the kitchen and Mom was taking out some vegetables to fix for dinner, and for no reason I could see, she suddenly dropped them on the floor and lit into Dad with her fists, screaming with rage. Moments later, he had her down on the floor, his own fists flailing away while she continued to shriek at him. It freaked me out with fright. I ran into the bedroom and crawled under the bed, sure I would be the next one to be beaten.

They were separated for a brief time after that — I believe I was about five at the time — but it wasn't for long. And when they did resume their rocky road together, the fighting went on and on, over all the years I can recall. That was one of the strange things in our home — my parents never slept together, and I have to wonder why they stayed together in the same house. In fact, Dad had his own separate bedroom, and it was strictly his. The rest of us, all four, slept sideways in the only other bed we had — Mom, with her feet on a clothes hamper because the bed wasn't wide enough for her to stretch out on, not with three growing children crowded into it with her.

Supporting that strange arrangement, they never kissed, never hugged, never touched each other or showed personal affection of any kind. On rare occasions, like maybe Christmas, Dad would sometimes make an attempt to reach out to her, but his overtures always met cold rejection. She didn't want to be touched! As for the screaming fights, I recall times when she would screech to the point where her vocal chords would simply cease to function. And as I grew older and threw my own screaming tantrums at school, I came to wish I were dead, because I didn't want to be like my mother.

Oddly enough, I pretended that life at home was normal, even as later years brought me the certain knowledge that our household wasn't exactly the haven of love it might have been. To say that I was a confused child is, I suppose, putting it mildly. Once, without thinking, I dashed unexpectedly into Dad's bedroom, only to glimpse him with no clothes on, ready to get dressed. It was of no importance to me; after all, I'd seen my brother unclothed many times, and this was my daddy — no big deal. But to him, it was!

"Get out of here, you nasty brat!" he shouted, grabbing for his shirt. "Who do you think you are, busting in here like that?"

I wanted to explain that I was only looking for something and hadn't known he was there, but the anger spewing out from every pore in his face told me I'd best get away while I could. "He hates me!" I thought to myself as I pulled the bedroom door shut behind me. "My dad hates me!" And then, as a logical sequence, "Everybody hates me! I wish I was dead!"

It wasn't all bad, of course. There were "ups" as well as "downs" from time to time. I learned to play alone much of the time, with our garage my favorite area. I'd take the treasures I had dug out of the trash cans next door and hide them away in the garage attic. When Mom would come out to check on me, I'd cover up. I didn't want her to know what I was doing, and I'm not sure she ever realized.

When I did play with the neighborhood kids, there was always difficulty of one sort or another. "You stay away from that turpentine!" These words of warning from my mother were a cinch to trigger trouble. Sure enough, little David from down the street had to have his stomach pumped after he took a solid swig of the stuff.

It wasn't any prize problem to me. After all, I ate bugs and flowers and almost anything else the neighbor kids told me to. I did it to be "in." I didn't want any of them to dislike me, so I went along with every suggestion they came up with. Like, "Hey, did you know that the middle of a flower is really good. You'll like it!" So I ate it, and pretended I found it as good as they said. It wouldn't have happened, if my parents had given me more confidence in myself. But there again, I should not entirely blame them. I was some kind of hellion, no matter the source.

Among the "up" times of childhood is the recollection of dashing with Paul out to Dad's truck when he'd stop by the house at lunchtime. We'd besiege him to take us to the beach, and occasionally he would. Paul and I would frolic along the strand while Dad fished, often totally ignoring us for hours at a time. These early good times at the beach set a pattern for my later escapades in that direction, for I really dug the sand and surf. These were our only family outings. Mom had no interest in camping trips or that sort of thing, so the infrequent forays to the ocean were highlights of an otherwise routine, boring, and often frightening existence.

Dad's employer had occasional family events, with Christmas standing out in my memory. There would be a special program and then Santa Claus gave out some really neat gifts and prizes — big, beautiful oranges and apples and candy and nuts that we didn't usually see at home. There would be nice gifts for all of us at Christmas-time, too. Dad and Mom were generous at that season, pointing up the probability that they really would have liked to do well by us kids, but they just didn't know how.

After I'd finished kindergarten in East Los Angeles, our family moved to Whittier, and for the next four years or so, I attended La Seda Elementary School — a period punctuated by both good and bad times for me. My special interest in arts and crafts, previously generated in kindergarten and Sunday school, blossomed; but here again, there were both pluses and minuses on the ledger.

On the plus side, I was provided the materials I could work with and enjoy at school, insuring continued interest in at least part of what went on. I enjoyed being complimented on my creative art work — a badly needed stimulus to an insecure youngster.

But overbalancing that feeling was the frustration I felt at home because I was limited to the simplest of tools there. I was lucky to get a small box of crayons and commonplace coloring book. My folks could not see beyond that basic need, while I was already into flights of fantasy about the great art works I was going to produce some day. I wanted paints, the kind I could use on occasion at school. Coloring books were for kids, and I was already seven or eight years old — long past that stage, as I saw it.

"What's the matter with you, JoJo? We spend our money and get you a nice box of colors and a book and you turn up your nose!" My mother's disgust was evident in the frown in her voice and on her face. "I just don't understand you!"

I knew it was useless, but I decided to try it once more. "Mom, I've told you, I want something more than an old coloring book. I want some water paints — like I use at school. I want to paint, to..."

"I never got any expensive paints when I was a kid!" My mother turned away in scorn. "Fact is, I never even had any colors at all. You better be thankful your father lets me buy you these."

Young as I was, I recognized the key word in her turn-off: *Expensive.* If paints were that expensive, I reasoned, how come the school could afford to provide them for us? So I amused myself with trying out new, and often weird, combinations of colors in the simple books they brought me, all the while dreaming of the day when I'd show them what real painting was all about.

There were infrequent occasions when Dad brought me colored pencils and other advanced art materials. Most of those showed up after I'd already passed that level of skill, so it didn't help.

I took out some of my frustrations in tomboy style. I dug acrobatics, especially playing on the bars at school. I was the tetherball champion — the best in school among both girls and boys. And I got into baton twirling. If I couldn't fulfill my dreams of being an artist, I'd be the champion baton twirler of all time. But that soon gave way to an all-consuming interest in roller skating.

As with my other athletic skills, I quickly developed dexterity on the skates, and for quite a period, roller skating was almost my entire life. I especially liked the short pleated skirts we girls wore to the rink. I'd spend hours ironing whichever skirt turned me on at the moment, and for a time, my dreams carried me to the realm of professional skating, and life was good.

It was during this time that other evidences of my "Want-what-I-want-when-I-want-it!" philosophy came to the forefront. I went through a phase of wanting to be like someone else, probably not unusual in a pre-adolescent girl. There was one particular girl whose short hair and single curl really sent me, and I wanted my hair exactly like hers. But that single curl simply refused to cooperate, and I got really hung up about it, while my screaming tantrums did less than nothing to solve the problem.

Meantime, as we children grew older, we were subjected more frequently to a subtle tug-of-war between our parents. Dad, when he had the chance, would get me aside and rail against my mother. "Your mom!" he would say, shaking his head and rolling his eyes. "She's really losing her marbles. I don't know how much longer we're going to be able to put up with her!"

I'd nod, trying to get by with saying as little as possible. And later, Mom would get me aside and say essentially the same thing about him. Such behavior on their part didn't exactly add to the already low opinion I had of myself, of my family, of my future.

A visit by my mother's sister and her family from New York didn't add anything to the family stability, and when they decided to stay in California permanently, Dad was fit to be tied. "That's all we need!" he exploded.

"Well, at least I'll have someone I can talk to once in a while!" was Mom's reaction, and it went on from there, although this time it stopped short of physical combat. I was confused. I thought my Aunt Ellen was pretty special, and I was glad she planned to stay.

Then, when I was in fifth grade, there was a paralyzing blow. "We're moving to La Puente," Dad announced at the dinner table one night.

I looked at Mom, expecting the usual outburst, but she just smiled at me and nodded. Obviously, she was in on this insidious plot to destroy me. Moving! I had my friends in Whittier, such as they were; I was in good at the skating rink; despite my lack of self-confidence, I was making it okay. But moving!

"Place has a really neat sidewalk!" Dad put in then. "You can skate all you want, JoJo."

Sidewalk skating wasn't exactly my thing. That was for the tiny tots. After all, I was a ten-year-old at this point, practically grown up.

"I won't go!" I announced firmly. Just like that.

For once, there wasn't any screaming fit from either of my parents. Worse — and much harder for me to take — they just ignored me. They packed up my things along with theirs, and they moved when the time came, and JoJo Myers, whether she wanted to or not, went along. But I didn't have to like it!

They did their best to help me adjust, up to a point, that is. They took me to the La Puente skating rink, but I soon discovered that all the "in" crowd rolled on a special kind of noiseless wheels. I stood it as long as I could.

"Mom, I've got to get some new skates, the kind with these special rollers," I finally announced, letting it all out at once. "Everybody's got them."

She glanced at me out of the corners of her eyes, a look I'd learned to distrust. "I'll speak to your father about it," she promised quietly.

"They're professional skates, Mom," I emphasized, giving her the brand name. "They're really cool!" I held my breath. I knew they were costly.

"Well, you've got a birthday coming up," Mom said. "We'll see what we can do."

I could hardly wait for October 20, my birthday, to roll around because I knew I'd be rolling myself from then on with my new skates. I was just getting started in the sixth grade in La Puente, and this would be a great way to make it with the "wheels" at school.

And sure enough, the box wrapped in birthday gaiety was just the right size for the professional roller skates I'd asked for. With eager fingers, I ripped off the wrapper, not even taking time to glance at the box as I tore its lid loose.

There, nestled inside the box, lay a pair of shoe skates, but one quick glance told me all I needed to know about them. These were not the pro skates I'd requested. They were not even a good imitation of them. These were a poor excuse for what I needed to be part of the gang at school and at the rink. I'd be laughed into a corner if I showed up with these.

With trembling fingers, I replaced the box lid I'd torn off. Then, not even mumbling a "Thank you" I wouldn't have meant anyway, I ran to my room, leaving the unwanted skates behind.

I could hear a vague, "Now isn't that the limit!" remark from Mom, but I couldn't have cared less. First, it had been the paints. Now the skates! The pattern was clear — whatever JoJo wanted, she'd settle for seconds, or else.

Burying my head in my pillow to fight back the tears, I clenched my lower lip between my teeth and made a vow, then and there.

"I'll never put on a pair of roller skates again as long as I live!" And I never have!

3

Teen-time —
Sousing, Shoplifting

Not long after I began attending Giano Junior High School in La Puente as a seventh grader, I was called to the office and told that the school district psychiatrist wanted to talk to me. I was shocked. I'd had a miserable year in the sixth grade, with little outlet for my restless energies — no skating, limited participation in other athletics, a continuing interest in art, but little opportunity to exercise it.

But my grades were adequate. I wasn't failing anything. And I couldn't see why the school shrink needed to dig into me. I saw myself much as any other seventh grader, having to put up with all kinds of unpleasantries dreamed up by long-since disillusioned teachers who couldn't think of anything better to do. So what?

"Do you love your mother?"

Of course I loved her. What idiot wouldn't love her own mother? What a stupid question! "Yeah." I sounded as bored as possible; maybe that would turn him off.

"How about your father?"

Another stupid question. "Yeah."

"Does your father love your mother?"

Now he was getting personal! I wanted to answer, "None of your business!" but I thought better of it. I shrugged. "Sure," I said, wondering just how much of a lie it really was.

The questions went on and on, and I made no effort to answer them with care. I just came out with the first thing that popped into my head.

"All right, JoAnn." The psyche-seeker started to put away his papers. "Thank you very much for your cooperation."

I nodded. He had to be putting me on. I hadn't cooperated at all — not since the first two or three questions. But it didn't matter. I didn't care. In the back of my mind, I had some plans. I'd watched some of the older girls ever since starting at Giano, and comparing them with the kids my own age, I'd come up with one conclusion: I belonged with the older group. All I had to do was find some way to get accepted — and then I'd show them all!

So I could care less what Mr. Psychiatrist thought about me or wrote down in his little black book. I knew surfing was the big thing with the older kids, and that meant whitening the hair to fit in better. And the next day after the shrink finished his probing, I gave my sandy hair the treatment, knowing this was a first step toward making the surfing scene.

"JoJo, what in the name-of-time did you do to your hair?" Mom's question didn't surprise me. I wondered, at that point, what I'd done myself. For instead of the bleached out strands I'd anticipated, my hair had turned sunset orange or bright carrot or sickly saffron. Take your pick.

I attempted to smile. "I tried to give it some color," I lied. "I — guess — it didn't turn out so good."

Mom shook her head sadly. "Well, it certainly didn't!"she said. "That's awful!"

I didn't know what to do to change it into something more acceptable. Besides, I wanted to be as far out as I could, so I left it like that, and secretly gloried in the glances it got, not caring whether they were envious or scornful. At least, I was getting some attention!

Among my seventh grade contemporaries was a girl my age named Cheryl, and I soon found out she had a couple of older sisters — Mikie and Janice — who were "with it" all the way. Mikie, in fact, was a little beyond where I was ready to go — as usually happens, her reputation had spread like wildfire around the school, apparently backed by her actual willingness to say "Yes!" to any boy with a proposition. At fourteen, Mikie was already treading a heavy trail. Petite, attractive, bubbling with personality, Mikie enjoyed the attention she got, but I could see that Cheryl and Janice looked down on her for what she was doing. I decided Janice was the one I really wanted to ditto. She was cool.

So after I got Cheryl to introduce me to Janice, I used any excuse

I could to be near her. She wasn't too ready to take me on at first. "Hey, kid, got a cigarette?" she asked one day when I was hoping to attract her attention.

She'd caught me unawares. I not only didn't have any cigarettes — I hadn't ever smoked one! But I'd soon remedy that, I promised myself. "I just smoked the last one," I lied, trying to smile. That night, I sneaked a half-dozen cigarettes into my purse from my mom's current pack, and the next day, before Janice could ask me, I dug one out and offered it to her.

"Thanks, kid. What did you say your name was?"

"JoJo," I told her. "Here — let me give you a light." With shaking fingers, I held the match for her, recalling how I'd seen my Mom do it. Then I put it to my own cigarette, and as the acrid taste of the smoke singed my tongue, I stifled the cough my throat wanted to loose.

"You're okay, Jo." Those were the most wonderful words I'd heard in years. I was "in." Janice, who was several steps further into what was happening than I was, had accepted me. From then on, I always had cigarettes, although I soon resorted to swiping small change from Mom's purse instead of taking the smokes from her package. I knew she wouldn't miss the change, but I was afraid she would realize her cigarettes were vanishing. There were plenty of machines where I could put in the coins and pick up the cigarettes — legal or not. So I did.

Janice knew the score, and she didn't seem to mind having me along. I think it was something of an ego trip for her, knowing this younger girl was patterning everything on what she did — something that neither of her sisters would do. I began wearing the same things Janice did, as close as I could. It was the time when medium checks were the thing, and Jan wore a red and white checked blouse that I absolutely fell in love with. I gave my mom the pitch.

"Mom, I've just got to have a checked blouse." I told her. "Everyone's wearing them, and they're not that expensive."

She nodded. One thing about her — she did her best to satisfy my needs and wishes when it came to clothes. "I'll see if I can't get you one the next time I'm out shopping," she promised.

It was a couple of days later that she handed me a sack. Her shy smile told me my dreams of a far-out checked blouse like Jan's were about to come true. I opened the sack slowly, savoring the thrill of the new acceptance I'd gain with the gang Janice ran with.

"Oh." Disappointment clutched at me, especially sharp because I suddenly realized I'd failed to tell Mom the color I wanted. "It's blue."

"It's checked!" Mom reminded me. "Isn't that what you wanted?"

I nodded sheepishly. "It's — fine," I said. And it was. The checks were just right. Only it wasn't exactly what Janice wore and exactly what Janice wore was what I wanted. But like so many times before, I'd have to make do. "Thanks, Mom!" I said. "Thanks a lot!"

That weekend, wearing the new blouse and some old jeans, I hitchhiked with Janice to West Covina. "It's where it's at!" Jan told me.

She was right. There were plenty of drive-in restaurants where we could pick up on guys and go from there. It was a whole new scene for me, and I could see that great times were in store. That night, in the car with a couple of fellows who picked up on us, I tasted beer for the first time, in between the cigarettes I was smoking, chain-style. But perhaps because she'd seen the way her sister, Mikie, had gone, Janice was careful to avoid any sex action, for both her and me. It was strictly kicks with smoking, drinking, and partying, and I looked forward eagerly to the next time we could go the same route.

The very next weekend, back in West Covina, we were invited to a party, and when we arrived, everyone was talking about the contest.

"What contest?" I asked.

"Guzzling contest — what else?" my new-found boy friend informed me. "Gonna enter?"

"Sure!" I said. "Why not?"

There was plenty of booze on hand to guzzle, it turned out, and when I was handed a fifth of vodka for my part in the contest, I didn't hesitate. I tipped up the bottle. Ignoring the burning taste that soon encompassed my mouth, I kept swallowing until I'd emptied the entire flask. Then I took a deep breath and was reaching for a second bottle, when a soon-to-be-familiar sound penetrated to my reeling ears.

"Jiggers — the fuzz!"

Our party was over, much more suddenly than it had begun. And my own personal party was just beginning, for it required only a few moments for the straight alcohol in my system to take over. By the time the cops were trying to load me into their car, I was really high.

"You're wonderful!" I told them, trying to get my arms around two of them at once. "I love you!"

They didn't seem to mind too much, but it didn't change anything. I spent the night in the cooler, and next morning, Mom and Dad had to come get me out. The love and attention they showed me were something new, because I wasn't used to having anyone feel sorry for me. But if they thought giving me extra interest and consideration might straighten the crooked path I'd taken, they were in for a big disappointment. I tried to outdrink a bunch of guys the very next weekend, with identical results: I was busted again!

This time, I happened to be wearing a pair of new shoes my mom had bought me, and somewhere along the way, I lost one of them. That made Mom mad!

Wiped out as I'd been the night before, I could remember that after I'd been handcuffed, I managed to slip the cuffs, and almost made it out the car window before we started for the police station. So I told Mom about it, and she laid it on the cops good.

"This girl had on brand new shoes when you picked her up!" she said. "And we're not leaving here till she has them on her feet — both of them!"

Mom could be pretty forceful when she wanted, and sure enough, one of the officers backtracked over the preceding night's trail, but to no effect. My one shoe was long gone. But strangely enough, Mom was mad at the cops, not at me. It was as if they were the ones really at fault.

From that time on, the pattern was regular as could be. Seldom a Friday night passed that JoJo Myers didn't get busted by the cops, drunk and disorderly. And Mom — with Dad along, too, on occasion — would come and get me. Then there'd be a go-round about how it shouldn't happen again and all that. A police matron counseled us, too. They insisted on trying to get the reason why I kept coming back, week after week. I didn't know. Neither did they. I think we all finally just accepted it. It was going to happen, and there wasn't much anyone could do about it. I was a fourteen-year-old hellhound, and that was the size of it.

Of course it all came down to a lack of love. I was not only intensely rebellious, I was constantly reaching for whatever escape from reality I could hope for. I refused to consider the consequences, and I was not ready to admit, at the time, the possibility that my home life might be different from that enjoyed by people around me. Feeling I lacked love and acceptance at home, I sought them outside the family circle. Any guilt feelings, any regrets I should have had were — by the very nature of my life — totally absent. In short, I went boozing and got drunk so the guys would like me. It was as simple as that.

The booze parties weren't always around West Covina. Some-times, we'd take off up into the San Bernardino Mountains and see how much beer we could put away. And of course there were some weekends when I'd get by without being hauled in by the gendarmes. But all in all, it was a period of perversity that set a pattern for the years that followed.

As time went on, my mother's patience wore thin — understandably. Super-wild as I was, I started going out at night during the week, impatient to wait for weekends, and Mom didn't want any part of that. So she'd scream at me the way she did at Dad, and I'd look for the chance to sneak away anyway.

More than once, she'd try to stop me. We'd have a crazy chase around the house before I'd manage to dodge out the door with her hot on my heels. She'd be yelling, and at the same time, I'd be cussing her out, using language I'd picked up from the gutter and from jail and from the smart-aleck friends I'd made. And often the next time I'd see her would be at the police station when she came to claim me after another bust.

Curfew violations, drunk and disorderly, playing hookey from school — they were all on my record. There came a time when the counselor warned me and my mom: "One more arrest and we'll have no choice. She'll have to go to Juvenile Hall." My mother winced, but I didn't think much about it. One place was the same as another, as far as I was concerned. If they didn't like me doing my thing, they knew what they could do about it, and if they put me in Juvenile Hall, maybe my mom wouldn't bug me so much for a while.

Down deep, of course, I wanted no part of Juvenile Hall, but there were still things to be done and I figured it was my time to do them. Like going with Cheryl and Mikie into one of the big department stores and trying on bathing suits in the dressing room, and forgetting to take them off and sneaking out with them on under our clothes. We were into surfing big, of course, and that meant we had to have more changes of personal cover than Mom and Dad would provide. An occasional snitch of a make-up compact or other small item was a regular incident, too.

We hadn't counted on being busted there, of course. Arrest for drunkenness or misconduct was one thing; stealing was another — as we discovered.

We'd pulled the make-up filch once too often, it turned out. We three were casually strolling out the front door, cigarettes in hand, and once outside, a heavy hand from behind was laid on my shoulder.

"You're under arrest!" Funny, those words had never sounded so ominous before, maybe because I'd always been drunk and couldn't care what happened to me. This time, there was no fooling around. On went the cuffs, and then Cheryl, Mikie, and I were paraded back through that store, hands shackled behind us for all to see, back to the security office to be held for the police. And the eye-shadow kits we'd "borrowed" were ungently removed from our bras by a woman security officer while we waited.

There was a stopover at the local slammer — I'd been there before — and I began to wonder just what was in store, because they spent a long time with my mom. I had dark visions of being shunted off into some foster home where I'd be mistreated and kicked around, and I began to wonder if life was really worth living when you had to go through all this misery. Then they finally came for me.

"You're on your way to Juvenile Hall, young lady," I was told. "Maybe that will pound some sense into that head of yours!"

Cheryl, I discovered, had been sent home with a warning, because she didn't have the heavy arrest record I did. And Mikie, it turned out, hadn't been seen pilfering anything, so she got off, too.

So I had to face Juvenile Hall by myself, and it wasn't exactly the most pleasant experience in the world. What I found were girls like me. They were trying to look like Mexican girls, and Mexican girls were trying to look like black girls, and an even larger number of blacks were trying to look like themselves. Many of these girls, I discovered, were far worse off than I was. We were all confused and looking for a way to put some sense into our lives and make people notice us.

"Who's that came to see you today?" Several of the others clustered around that second afternoon.

"Oh, that was my mom and dad," I explained. "They always show up when I'm in trouble."

"Hey, that's far out!"

"Wow — my old lady wouldn't come to see me at my funeral, let alone here! You're lucky, Jo!"

"Yeah — like the last thing I heard was, 'I ain't gonna have nothing to do with you no more!' "

I was feeling pretty sorry for myself, but I realized that others might be lots worse off than I was. But I was the youngest in the bunch, and when the matrons decided to put me in a solitary cell instead of the dormitory because I was going to the bathroom so often, I really felt afraid, alone, and friendless. I toughed it out for several nights, and then came a time when I couldn't stand it any longer.

I cried for a long time, first to myself. Then, in final despair, I dredged up out of my earlier church memories the fact that people with troubles called out to God, whoever He was.

"Oh, God!" I cried, and it was a frantic plea into anywhere. "Please get me out of here!" And I burst into uncontrollable sobbing until one of the matrons came and talked to me for more than half an hour. It didn't help; when she left, I cried myself to sleep.

Nothing unusual happened the following day, but the day after that — I'd been in the hall about a week by then — my Mom showed up. They brought her directly to my cell.

"They're going to let you come home with me, JoAnn," she said quietly. "I hope you've learned a lesson."

"Oh, thank God!" The words just popped out.

"What did you say?" I'd taken Mom by surprise with that outburst.

Embarrassed, I tried to cover it up. "Oh, nothing. It's about time they let me go!"

She looked at me sternly, but I was lost in thought. Maybe there was something to this business of God and all that; I'd called on Him to get me out of here, and I was getting out. It was an exciting thought, but one I soon lost track of, with all the exhorting to straighten up and fly right and all that. I could wish, now, that I'd given more thought to the possibility that God did answer my cry into the night, that He might be available for help and guidance in other ways, too. But my thoughts were elsewhere; I was willing to accept the fact of my release, and how it might have come about was of no concern.

I didn't need to be warned to stay square, however. I really wanted to do it. We didn't have to go to court, and after some counseling, they let us go. And I had every intention of hanging in there on the straight and narrow from then on.

But staying around the house and listening to Mom and Dad yell at each other every night wasn't exactly a delightful kind of picnic. I soon got bored with the whole setup. Besides, I could see Jeannette going off with her friends and having fun, and just how much Monopoly can you play with your ten-year-old brother before you start climbing the walls? Much as I loved him, I couldn't help being impatient to do things I thought were more fun.

So it was back to the old haunts again, though I will say I was a little more careful now. I'd been busted just once too often, and I could see there had to be ways around that sort of foolishness. So I resorted to other foolishness, instead.

Nogales High Schol, where I was now a freshman, had a thing about short skirts...but so did I. I grooved on them; the school frowned. So every day I'd go to school in my short skirt, and I'd get sent to the principal's office right away, where the vice-principal would actually measure the length of my dress and send me home for something more suitable. Then the very next day, I'd show up again with the short skirt, and we'd go through the same silly routine again.

I didn't make many classes, of course, for I didn't always return to school after being sent home to dress differently. As often as not, I'd ditch the rest of the day, either before or after I went home for "suitable clothing."

On one such day, I decided to ditch to go to the beach, and I didn't bother going home for a longer skirt first. I knew some of my girl friends were planning a beach trip that day, too, and since I was afraid I might get caught before I could get away to join them, I didn't hesitate when I saw a truck pull up at a stop sign there by the school.

"Hey!" I said to the swarthy-looking driver. "Could you take me to Valley Boulevard? I'm going to meet my girl friend there and we're going to go to the beach!"

He reached over and opened the door. "Hop in!" he said, so I did.

It wasn't long until I began to figure I'd blown it. Because we weren't heading for Valley Boulevard — not by any route I'd ever taken, anyway. He just kept driving, leering over at me and smiling once in a while. I wanted to jump out, but I didn't dare. I didn't know what might happen.

"Are we — on the way to Valley Boulevard?" I finally asked in a timid voice, barely above a whisper.

"Sure," he said, a little too heartily. "We're just taking the long way around."

He kept on driving, and I saw that we were getting away from the city area, into open country where the only break in the green of the hills was an occasional housing tract under construction. And one of those, indeed, was where we first stopped.

"Come on!" my chauffeur said. "Want to show you to some of the boys."

Still fearful, I accompanied him as he led me by the hand to where workmen were pounding nails into the housing frames and digging ditches for the gas and water lines.

"Hey guys, look what I got!" he boasted. If I'd had a brain in my head, I'd have run to some of them then and there, seeking safety in numbers, but I really wasn't aware of what was happening. The fellows on the job laughed and nodded and tossed in a few off-color remarks, but still I didn't tumble to the seriousness of the situation. And finally, the truck driver led me back to his rig.

"Hey," he said, "how about a little drink? Got me some vodka and O-J here."

"No, thank you," I said, shivering. I was beginning to panic now. This was a lot more than I'd bargained for when I asked for a lift to Valley Boulevard.

"Come on!" he urged, and there was an undertone of ugliness in his tone. "Drink it!"

With shaking fingers, I took the cup and downed the screwdriver combination. The truck jerked into motion, and I saw that he was fortifying himself with a stiff jolt of juice while he drove.

Almost before I knew it, we were in a deserted area, no sign of civilization in sight. I wanted to jump from the truck and run, but I could only sit there, paralyzed with fright.

"Okay, baby, take 'em off!"

"Wh-what?"

"Strip 'em, kid! We're gonna have some fun!"

I'd gotten drunk with the fellows. I'd made out up to a point. I'd teased them with short skirts and tight sweaters. But I'd never really gotten into the sex scene. Now, I realized, this man — this monster — was telling me to take off my clothes. His intentions were obvious.

"Hurry up — get with it!" He took another pull from his bottle, then reached over and tore my blouse open, ogling my bra-less chest.

"Come on, get 'em off!" he urged, his breathing heavy. I complied. I was suddenly sitting there naked beside this man with the glittering eyes and crooked teeth in the cab of a truck in the middle of nowhere.

What happened then is best forgotten. For the record, I was not raped. He was a pervert. He was sick...beyond imagination. When he had satisfied himself and told me to put my clothes back on, I was bleeding in three places — my lips, where I'd bitten them in frantic desperation, and my breasts.

Without a further word, he drove me to a street where cars occasionally whizzed by, pushed me out, and went his way. I was dressed now, of course, but I sat by the side of that street and tried to bring my senses together for a long time before I finally got up and timidly held up my hand to seek a ride back toward home. I'd hitchhiked plenty of times with never a thought of possible consequences. Now, I knew the terror that could happen.

Somehow, I got home. Only then did the true horror of it fasten me in its unrelenting grip. This was the worst of all. There was no one to confide in, no one I could talk to. I had been ravished and I could tell no one.

My mother...my sister...strangers both! I could only entomb my grief and suffering within myself. This was almost worse than the savagery I'd undergone!

4

Degeneracy —
Drugs, Rape

I had to tell someone! At fifteen years, I simply was not prepared to bottle up inside me what had happened in the desolate stretches of wherever. For no particular reason — I'd certainly never been especially friendly with her — I chose Donna, my sister's friend who lived a couple of houses away from us. I went there when Jeannette, my sister, was gone.

"Where's your mom?" I asked suspiciously, glancing around to be sure we were alone.

Donna shrugged her narrow shoulders. "Off shopping, I guess. Why — what's up?"

Again looking around to make sure no one else was in sight, I opened my blouse and blurted out the general details of my encounter, omitting some of the more sordid aspects of it. I was in tears by the time I finished; only then did I realize that Donna being older wasn't letting herself overreact. She simply listened stoically to the entire report, with no interruption, no comment. Instantly, I regretted having told her, but I had to tell someone! I was only a kid.

Donna tossed off that "So what?" shrug again, and her words frightened me. "What'd your mom say?"

I shivered, hanging my head. "I didn't tell her." The words were a mere whisper.

"She'd probably flip." Donna nodded. "You're not hurt, JoJo. Might as well forget it. Ain't no big thing."

No big thing. Maybe not — to someone who hadn't undergone that fear-filled ordeal. I didn't know what to say now. Slowly, I rebuttoned my blouse. I don't know what I'd expected from

Donna, but certainly I hadn't looked for this total lack of interest or sympathy.

So I went back home, ashamed that I'd had to unburden myself to someone who couldn't care less what happened to me. I still needed someone to talk to. But there wasn't any *someone* around for me.

I could have — obviously, I should have — profited by my bitter experience at least to the point of changing my ways. But I didn't. When I went back to school, I wore one of those same short skirts that sent me to the principal's office on a regular schedule. And knowing from prior conversations that Janice and Cheryl and a couple of the other girls were beach-bound again that day, I joined them as usual. But it wasn't a good day for me. My tightly stretched bikini bra, while it covered the areas of laceration, made me terribly uncomfortable. I was glad when our usual hitchhiking thumbs got us safely home that night.

It wasn't long after that when the school authorities gave up on me, and transferred me from Nogales High to Continuation School — the place for the incorrigibles who simply wouldn't conform to normal requirements. It didn't mean much to me. One school was as bad as another. I could come up with straight "F's" for grades at Continuation just as well as at Nogales.

There were more weekend escapades, and I was busted again and again — drunk and disorderly. There was one matron at the jail where I usually ended up, who had a standard line. "If you don't stop this messing around, you're going to turn into a prostitute!"

"Oh, sure!" I said. It sounded so ridiculous.

Fear seemed their only tool. Whatever they said or did, it was aimed at trying to scare me into not doing all the things that got me into trouble. It was a negative approach that did less than no good at all.

Then came the time when even Continuation School couldn't keep up with me, and my parents were called in by the authorities for consultation.

"There's no choice left," was the ultimatum. "We're going to have to put JoAnn in a foster home — unless you have some relatives where you can place her." There was a pause, to let this sink in. "The situation here is simply — untenable!"

We were in the principal's office at the school, but the speaker
was a matron from the county jail where I'd ended up so many
times. She looked at my father, but as usual, he wasn't about to get
involved, leaving it up to my mother to decide.

"Well, she does have an older cousin in Elsinore," mother
ventured. "I suppose she might go there."

I hid the smile that wanted to touch my lips. Living with
Carolyn, whose mother was my mother's sister, might not be a
total blast, but it would at least be different. I had a lot of respect
for her. She had seven children, all tiny, and at twenty-six, she was
raising her family by herself. I had a couple of quick thoughts that
Mom wasn't doing her niece any favors by foisting incorrigible me
off on her, but if that was the way she wanted it...

The matron nodded. "Check it out with her," she said, handing
my mother a form to fill out. "If she agrees, we'll need the
information on this sheet." With a discouraged nod in my
direction, she closed another shoddy chapter in my life. "I hope it
helps!"

It was a totally new scene at Elsinore, a resort-type town on the
edge of a small artificial lake. Carolyn was cool about taking
charge of me, and I reacted the same way. She didn't lay down any
silly rules, and I didn't need any — for a time. I dug in and helped
around the house, and aided with the children. I actually came to
know a little about happiness — something new and strange in my
life. More than anything else, I was afraid of letting Carolyn down,
so things went well for a time.

But there was a restless streak inside me that wouldn't be denied,
and after I'd stayed out of school a few weeks, Carolyn decided
she was neglecting her duty, and it was time for me to go back.
That suited me fine, for it gave me the chance to meet some
persons in my own age group, and that meant getting into the party
scene and all that went with it.

And if I'd been a hellion at home, I was a harebrained daredevil
in Elsinore, once I got my feet on the ground. The best way to
attract attention, I found, was to go all-out weird — so I did. Once,
I went for a beach stroll along the lake-edge with a bird cage on
my head, worn like a hat. I would march out into the middle of
the street, with its heavy weekend traffic, hold up my hand like a
cop, and then approach the stopped and puzzled driver.

"Got a cigarette?" I'd ask casually. It was a real flip-out.

At the lake's edge, I'd hitch a ride on passing boats — a good way to get going with guys. Sometimes, I'd just stay in the boat, smoking, drinking, and leading on whatever fellows might be riding it; other times, I'd borrow someone's water skis and have a real ball skimming over the water.

Before the authorities had delivered their ultimatum to my parents, I'd had a few dates with a guy named Mike, and it was with him that I got my first taste of sex. As with drinking, I did it only because I felt I had to, to hang on to Mike. He'd picked me up one night, and he came back the next day, which blew my mind because I was used to being dropped with no further interest. So we had a few dates, but once I'd given in to his urging, that was it. I never saw him again after the one time.

And after that time, I wanted to bury myself somewhere. I felt absolutely awful; I hated myself for what I had done. I felt guilty and I also felt turned off, because I found the experience anything but enjoyable.

Yet, because I felt I had no choice if I wanted to stay popular, I was going all-out with guys who were ready and willing at Elsinore. And before long, Carolyn began to loosen up and take life a little less seriously, too.

She tried to keep me in line at first. "You got drunk last night!" she'd accuse me.

Wide-eyed and innocent, I'd protest, saying, "No, I didn't!"

"Oh yes you did!" she'd say, and finally it got so there was no hassle. Like my mother, Carolyn just seemed to accept my behavior as inevitable.

There were a lot of motorcycle enthusiasts in the Elsinore area, and Carolyn decided — understandably, because she'd been tied down to the kids so long — she'd like to be a biker, too. So I'd babysit the children, giving her the chance to get away for overnight trips, or perhaps an all-day trek to the nearby mountains. Naturally, I wanted to get into the biker scene, too, so I started wearing a Levi jacket and pants, and it was easy to get anywhere I wanted to — just go down to the corner and hitch a ride with the first unattached biker to wheel down the street.

In tiny Elsinore bikers weren't my only new experience. I got really turned on there to whites, which contained speed, and that was for me, because it loosened me up. The inhibitions that made me insecure, unhappy, and afraid of the world were all gone. So from that point, drugs became very much a part of my life. It wasn't just the speed, either. I dropped LSD for the first time, and the results were close to disaster.

I'd developed a bad reputation in that little community, so when Dan — a guy with an equally bad reputation — picked up on me, it was sort of a matter of pride. Together, we'd show them all! This particular night, Dan slipped me a tab of acid, and before long, I began to experience some pretty weird psychedelic effects. Making out with Dan was not especially exciting, but watching a beautiful tapestry change its patterns into all sorts of wild color combinations was something else.   Everything around me changed...and kept changing. I was transported into the endless reaches of nowhere, and my mind was pulled in a dozen directions at once.

I kept reaching out, trying to grasp some sort of reality, but it wasn't there.   Finally, it occurred to me that I might be going insane, I was so flipped out, but I did have the presence of mind to know that Carolyn's house was the place where I belonged. I managed to put enough words together to ask Dan to take me there.

I walked in, the world reeling crazily around me like a torrent of inside-out rainbows. I wanted to tell Carolyn about my LSD trip, but I was still hallucinating, and I simply couldn't get things into focus. I tried drinking some beer, but it didn't seem to help.

Everything was still rolling around and over and under me in a fantastic array of spooky colors, and I just couldn't get it all together.   Now I was sure I was going insane, and finally I managed to get my problems across to her.

"Look, get me in the hospital. Get the cops to come pick me up, anything!" I begged. "I'll even get busted — anything to get rid of this weird feeling!"

"I'll call the doctor," Carolyn agreed, and I relaxed a little.

But the doctor wasn't much help. "What'd she take?" he asked Carolyn.

I'm not sure I'd told her, but she made a good guess. "LSD, I think," Carolyn said. "She's really out of it! You want to talk to her?"

I shook my head violently. I wasn't about to talk to him. I couldn't trust myself to talk to anyone at this point.

Carolyn listened awhile, and then, nodding her head, hung up.

"What'd he say?" It was a major effort to push the words out.

"He said, 'When she starts climbing the walls and screaming, call me again!'" Carolyn informed me. "He thinks you'll live through it."

"Oh — wow! Thanks a lot!" I told her. And I stumbled to my bedroom, the world reeling around me.

By the next day, my mind had cleared, but I still felt wrung out. And Carolyn, being older, was trying to pound some sense into my head.

"JoJo," she said, sitting beside my bed, "you can have a better life. You don't have to take dope to make it!"

And she went on, recalling how much fun it was being out in the snow in New York, before her family had moved to California. She made it sound really exciting.

"Really?" I said, afraid to believe life could actually be that way. I'd searched for some sort of happiness for all my sixteen years, and I'd never found it. I wasn't sure it existed. I sensed that Carolyn had some of the inner peace I sought, and I wondered, "What is it she's got?" But I was too timid to ask. By now, the effects of the things I'd taken had worn off enough that I was the same frightened, insecure person I'd always been, when I wasn't high on booze or pills or acid or whatever.

I suppose that by this time, it was apparent to everyone that JoJo Myers wasn't making any changes for the better at Elsinore, and she might as well go back to La Puente. In any case, after several months Mom seemed to want me back home, so back I went, and picked up at Continuation School where I'd left off. I'd only been busted once in Elsinore — a record for me — but I'd broadened my realm of experience considerably. Almost immediately, Janice and I started a regular routine of hitting the spots in Hollywood, where we could get all the whites we wanted, and stay high on speed. I really dug the whites because they seemed to be a perfect key to opening me up.

The hippie scene was just getting started at that time, and both Janice and I turned on to it. We'd get in with those Hollywood freaks, and we'd get high on pills or booze or both and take things as they came.

If I'd dressed weird before, I was super-weird now: velvet pants with bell bottoms and jeweled buttons down the sides; silk blouses in a variety of colors; velvet capes, all trimmed with lots of jewelry and beads; and my hair bushed out...the freakier the better.

We'd hit the night clubs, the coffee houses, the other spots on the Sunset Strip, getting stoned on whatever was available, picking up on guys, and staying out all night or all weekend.

I'd gone to school with black kids, and I'd lived in Juvenile Hall with black girls, and as far as I was concerned, blacks and Chicanos and Orientals and everyone else were one and the same. I didn't pay any attention to their color.

There was a black guy who lived across the street from us who often gave me rides to Hollywood. People really liked Big John. He was a leader type, and he was really with it. Taking whites and drinking wine was my thing at that time, and Big John would always come through when I asked him. It was he who first introduced me to grass, adding a new experience to my growing stock. Even my mom liked Big John. I think she trusted him, unaware that even though my relationship with him was more like brother-sister, he was into drugs pretty heavy.

I suppose it would be logical to wonder why, somewhere along the way, I didn't run into someone "straight" who could influence me in better directions. The reason I didn't was because I had an overwhelming distaste for what I termed "the establishment." Possibly because of my own experiences with the skates, colors, and other hangups at earlier times, I hated every holiday, including my own birthday. As far as I was concerned, Christmas, Easter, and the like were only establishment rip-offs, and I wanted no part of their traditional celebrations. On the other hand, the hippie scene, being anti-establishment, seemed to hold just what I was looking for.

With the hippies came love-ins at Griffith Park in Los Angeles, and that was a drama I could dig. It was free love all the way, and I liked getting into my freaky costumes to attract all the attention I could...see-through yellow pants, anything that was different or far-out. And everyone around me was the same way. There'd be groups of strolling musicians, playing guitars and singing and getting together. If you bothered to look, you'd see couples unconcerned with the world around them, responding to physical desires whenever the mood struck them.

With Big John one weekend, I talked my sister Jeannette into going to a Griffith Park love-in — unusual, because she was straight. Once there, I got into the wine bottles to get myself loosened up, and apparently I got into more than I realized, for I have no memory of what happened later — just the various reports I got from Jeannette and others.

It seems Jeannette started looking for me late in the day, and being unable to spot me, wandered to some of the more remote reaches of the park. Attracted by what appeared to be some sort of scramble, she discovered a group of guys (she claimed sixty of them, which had to be an exaggeration of considerable proportions), all trying at the same time to get to someone for sex action. And I was that someone!

I was naked. My beautiful outfit Mom had bought me had been ripped to shreds, and there I was on the ground, scratched and bruised, but because so many were all trying to get to me at once, no one was making it.

Jeannette screamed, but the hippies around her were unconcerned. She looked for a forest ranger, but could find no one of authority to help. Finally, one man responded, looked to where she was pointing in desperation, and listened to her frightened words.

"I'll go get her!" he said, and he did. He just waded in and started pulling the guys away, and finally got to me. From somewhere (maybe some of my attackers had left them) he produced an extra pair of trousers and helped me get into them. They kept falling off, they were so large, but he helped me hold them on. He led me to a ranger's car nearby, pushed me inside and told me to lock the doors. It was a good thing, because some of the guys came back a little later and began pounding on the windows. Petrifying!

Big John had disappeared by now, so Jeannette called Mom, and she came to take us home. I didn't really know where I was or what was going on until next morning, when I woke to a horrendous headache and heard my sister talking to my mother in the adjoining room.

"Mom, you should have seen it," Jeannette was saying. "It was just horrible!"

I suddenly realized I had scratches and bruises over much of my body, and aches in various spots aside from my splitting hungover head. "What?" I wondered. "What happened to me?"

But Jeannette wasn't through. "You better do something about that girl!" she said. "She's nothing but a whore!"

I shuddered. Who in the world did Jeannette think she was, talking that way about her own sister?

"Yeah, I know, I should do something." I could sense from Mom's voice that she was really worried, but I knew from experience that nothing would come of it. I dreaded to hear what had happened, hated myself for having let myself in for whatever it was. I wanted to die. But I couldn't. Underneath, deep down, there was a recurring fright I kept trying to push out of my confused consciousness: If what Jeannette said was true, would I become pregnant...or diseased...or something worse? I simply shrunk from thinking about it.

Later, my mother and sister insisted that we go to the police station to file charges against the attackers, but it was wasted effort.

The attitude, understandably, was, "Well, you asked for it! You can't find the guys. You can't even remember what they looked like. What can you do?" They were right. There was nothing we could do.

But while that brief experience turned my sister off love-ins for life, it didn't bother me all that much. I was back at Griffith Park the very next weekend!

About that time, Big John started going with Jennie, a white girl who was a few years older than I, and I really liked running around with Jennie. There were no more problems in Griffith Park, and Jennie and I started making the Hollywood area together, turning on with speed. I was sixteen, but the way I dressed, I could easily pass for older, and we'd pick up on anyone we could.

One morning about two o'clock, we decided to head for home, and up went the thumbs as usual. I remember thinking, "We better be careful who we get in a car with." There was always the question of my being under age, and if a plain clothes cop came along, I could get busted all too easily.

A car pulled over, responding to our signal, and we saw that there were a couple of guys in it. "Two of them, two of us," I thought. "No problem."

So we got in, chatted in friendly fashion for awhile, and having told the guys where we lived, figured they'd take us all the way home. We were wrong.

We started taking back streets, ending up behind an old apartment. When the guys stopped the car, as though by prearranged planning, six more fellows came running up to it. The two who'd picked us up just faded from sight, and Jennie and I could see trouble coming quick. One of the guys had a knife with a blade that must have been at least fourteen inches long.

"You gonna get it, Whitey!" It was immediately evident what they meant. "You gonna get it or you dead!"

"Please!" Jennie pleaded. "She's only fifteen years old!"

It didn't matter. This time, the rape was real. Somewhere along the way, Jennie managed to voice more protest. "Why are you doing this?"

The reply was short and to the point from the same black who had called us Whitey. "Because you murdered our father — Martin Luther King!" The religious leader had been killed only a few days before, April 4, 1968.

When it was over, our attackers suddenly seemed to have a change of heart. "She only fifteen?" One of them pointed to me, his eyes on Jennie.

"You better believe it!" Jennie said, dropping a year off my life.

"Oh — sorry about that. We didn't know!"

It was no excuse, of course, but apparently they figured a young girl like me could cause problems. They melted into the night, and Jennie and I were left to feel our way back to whatever civilization we could find.

The speed I'd taken was wearing off, and coupled with the terrifying experience we'd gone through, it was too much for me. We were walking down a well-lighted street, and suddenly I was sure they were after me again, and I started running. I could hear the bloodcurdling sound of heavy footsteps behind me, and I ran faster than ever.

"Wait, JoJo! It's only me!" The voice was familiar, but it only frightened me more. "Slow down!"

I kept running, still hearing those footsteps pounding after me.
And finally, Jennie caught up with me, grabbed my shoulder and
turned me around so I could see her. I fell into her arms.

"Get me some speed!" It was all I could think of to say.

5

Constant Run —
to Suicide, to Juvenile Hall

Once again, I faced the problem of having to bottle up a bitter experience. Jennie, of course, had shared it with me, but I'd already unloaded on her, and there was simply no one else I could tell. Deep inside, a special terror was gnawing at me: What if I was pregnant? I'd never bothered to worry about that when I'd made my own choice, but a rape-result pregnancy was something else. All I could think of was to bury my woes in speed or anything else I could get my hands on.

One of the guys I was dating off and on at that time was called Mouse. Though I couldn't turn to him with my personal problems, I could look to him to help me forget the past, in more ways than one.

So on the next trip to Hollywood, Jennie and I headed for the pad where Mouse was supposed to be staying. When I found him in the bedroom with another girl, I guess I just flipped out. I knew where he kept his stash, so I grabbed a tab of acid and dropped it. The stuff was heavy — white lightning, liberally laced with speed — but I was ready for it, I thought; I needed it!

And this turned into some sort of trip! It was a real bummer. I literally went to hell and there was nothing sure about my coming back, for awhile.

I was sitting on the couch in the living room of the apartment, waiting for Mouse to show up from the bedroom, and I suddenly decided I wanted a drink of water. I got up to get it — an ordinary action that even the average drunk could accomplish — but I couldn't get it on. Someway, I couldn't figure out how to walk to the kitchen or the bathroom for the drink I wanted. It was weird! I walked around in circles, but things weren't going sideways and backwards and every which way with the psychedelic colors I'd seen on my first LSD trip. Instead, things looked perfectly normal, but I simply could not sort them out.

I decided to sit down and figure it out, but I didn't know how to sit down! I could not relate to my surroundings — not in any way at all. I was really tripping out, and Jennie, realizing how far out of it I was, began to get worried.

"What am I going to do?"

Through the haze of my mist-filled mind, I could sense Jennie's concern for me. It dawned on me that maybe Mouse could help. So I managed to stumble back to the bedroom, where the girl he was with had some harsh words for me.

"Get lost!" she yelled. "I came all the way up here from Long Beach to see him, and if you think..."

I didn't wait to hear the rest of whatever she had to scream.

Everyone was against me — everyone but Jennie — and there was just one thing to do. I'd turn them all loose. They wouldn't be burdened with JoJo Myers again. I turned away, and somehow found the outside door, opening on the second level balcony walkway to the apartment. There was an iron grillwork at the edge of the balcony, and I didn't waste any time getting over to it. The stone patio beneath looked inviting, as though it were extending open arms to me, just waiting for me to jump into them.

Inside the apartment, Jennie had turned on the record player, and I could hear a Beatles song vaguely filtering through the air, urging me to spread my wings and float down to the rock facing below. I felt as though I was in a never-ending infinity. There was no longer any existence of time. I was suspended in hell, in a void where there was nothing, yet there was everything. I poised to leap.

Suddenly, with a strength I wouldn't have believed possible, Jennie had me by the arm, dragging me back into the apartment.

"No way JoJo!" she was crying. "No way!"

The record was still going. "Ah...ah...ah...ah...ah..." It was becoming more and more intense, a never-ending song that was getting to me. Again, I was in infinity, where time and everything else ceased to exist. I could not seize on any kind of thought — ideas eluded me, and I felt like I was just sagging in space. And then, a paralyzing idea did penetrate: Maybe I was dead! Was this what it was like to be dead?

Through the blur of nothingness, I could suddenly see two indistinct faces — my mother, I was sure she was one. The other, I couldn't be sure — yes, it was...it was my brother. I reached out to them, wanting to bring the reality of their beings into my arms for reassurance. I reached and reached...but I could not connect. Always they seemed just beyond my out-thrust fingertips. I began to cry. I felt they were gone forever, because they were there but I could not touch them. Gone forever!

Through the tears that obscured those shadowy faces, I now saw walls of cotton white — walls that seemed to creep ever closer to me. And then I felt it — a hard slap on the face, and from somewhere in the distance I could hear the harsh-voiced nurse yelling at me.

"Come out of it! Come out of it!"

Come out of what? What is there to come out of? It was a supreme effort to put those feeble thoughts together. What was it I was supposed to come out of?

Another slap, and the air around me suddenly cleared. There was Jennie, hand hovering to strike again. Jennie! It wasn't the nurse after all. And this was Mouse's apartment — not a hospital!

"Come on, Joey. Come out of it!"

Jennie's words were clear this time, not trailing in out of a wraithlike fog as before. "Okay, Jennie," I said dreamily. "I love you!" And I reached out to verify the reality of her being. It felt good to be able to touch her and to know it was really her sitting there beside me.

I was alternately with it and out of it the rest of that night. My tripping out ended next morning as abruptly as it had begun, and all of us wrapped up and headed to Griffith Park for the love-in scheduled that day. As usual, I'd worn my black velvet cape, held together at the neck with a big antique brooch I'd picked up somewhere. My pants were a wild flower print, made of drapery satin, and fashioned with bell bottoms and sparkly buttons up the sides. The blouse was matching material, and with my black boots and bleached bushy hair — all ratted out to take up twice its normal space — I must have been quite a sight. I had a jeweled headband, too, plus tons of make-up, mostly on the eyes. It's a wonder I could even see out.

The lesson I should have learned from my prior Griffith Park love-in experience should have made me wary of ever getting near such an event again, but it seemed to have the opposite effect. I went to every love-in I could find, and fortunately, I didn't ever duplicate my earlier dilemma.

Bad though it was, life went on, and there came a Friday night when Janice and I spent the night in Hollywood, then walked along Sunset Boulevard the next morning. She had a leather purse which I really dug, so I voiced my feelings.

"Hey, let me carry your purse, huh?" I could always open up with Janice, no matter if I was high on speed or wine or whatever.

"Sure, Joey. Be my guest!"

And almost as if that were their cue, a couple of uniforms in a black-and-white police cruiser rolled up beside us. "Hey, girls, whatcha doing?"

There was no cause to panic. We were minding our own business. "Taking a walk," Janice told them. "Anything wrong with that?"

"You been out all night?"

We shrugged that one off. "What difference does that make?" I said. "My mom said it's okay for me to..."

"What your mom says is okay and what's really okay may be two different things," one of the cops interrupted me. "You girls better come with us." Reluctantly, we climbed into the black-and-white.

Busted! We could tell from snatches of conversation that followed on the way to the station that they thought we were runaways. I knew there was nothing they really had on us, so this would be just another free ride. We'd be back on the streets in a couple of hours.

At the station house, however, things took a new turn. Janice had apparently forgotten — and I hadn't known — she'd tucked some marijuana into her compact somewhere along the way. When they found that, the reaction was sharp and quick.

"Juvenile Hall for her!" one of the cops said, nodding toward me.

"Hey, wait a minute!" Janice put in. "That's my purse. I'm the one who had the grass. Bust me, not her!"

But they'd have no part of it. The pot was in my possession when we were picked up, and that meant I was responsible. I checked back in to Juvenile Hall that afternoon, quite an extended time from my earlier first visit, but I found it hadn't changed much. Some new faces among my companions, perhaps, but the same old tired supervisors and the same old tired walls and sparse furnishings and crumby atmosphere.

They let me cool my heels for two weeks, and then I came up for a court hearing. Once there, I must have gone into shock, for I have no specific memory of what happened, though I've been told about it. I'm not sure what triggered my outburst, but I ended calling the judge a name straight out of the streets.

That did it! A cop or a marshal on duty grabbed me, picked me up, and actually threw me against the wall, knocking my head up against it. I guess I'd pulled a pretty big no-no!

"Three months in Juvenile Hall! Maybe you can learn to behave!"

It didn't bother me especially. Life was a drag any way you looked at it. If there was a better way of life, I certainly didn't know about it. I hadn't been able to discover it. And while I knew I'd miss the things that were key elements in my life — cigarettes, booze, speed, that sort of thing — if it gave the authorities such a big charge to coop me up for ninety days, so what? They weren't going to change anything, as far as I was concerned.

The next day, my probation officer started really getting on my case, going on about my reading off the judge and calling him a bad name. I got pretty sore, but the things I said were said to myself instead of to her. I'd learned that much the first time around. What I wanted to say was, "So I called the judge a bad word — so what? You can just go jump in the lake. I'm stuck here in Juvenile Hall, and there's nothing we can do about it so what's your big trip?"

"Your Mom's really worried about you. You shouldn't be a bad girl!"

That almost did it! But that was part of the big problem. I could never bring myself to talk about the way things were at home. So I just went on hating the system and the society that put probation officers over us who could no more relate to the problems faced by juvenile offenders than a head shrinker could fix a broken leg. They were phony and we all knew it!

The routine at Juvenile Hall was something else, compared with what I was used to. We'd be jarred out of bed at 5:00 A.M., sent to the kitchen to cook breakfast — and I certainly wasn't used to that! I'd walk around half-asleep.

But after the chow call and clean-up, it was even worse, for there was nothing to do. It was like jail. It did have one good effect, however — it made going to school, even the Juvenile Hall school we had to attend, a pleasure just because it was different. I even went to church on Sundays, to relieve the boredom of an unhappy existence. But it did no good; it was empty; it seemed there was more talk of who was getting out when than any real seeking of the Lord's blessings. Apparently, the person doing the talking didn't know God. The singing, I recall, did touch me somewhat, but it was limited and talentless and hence had no lasting effect. I heard and felt no conviction whatsoever concerning God's love. So I listened to the services with half-an-ear, my mind occupied with other things I found more important.

There was plenty of time to think. And although my parents would visit on Saturday mornings, and I would cry and Mom would cry and we'd have quite a sobbing session, after they'd gone I'd review some of the things that had happened and wonder what the weeping jag was all about.

I'd think back to the time when I'd have liked to have some of my friends visit me at the house, but I was always afraid to. I never knew what Mom would say next, and I was fearful that I'd be embarrassed beyond belief.

After I'd gotten into trouble enough times that it was a regular routine, Mom always put the blame on everyone else. "You'd never be where you're at if it wasn't for those girls you hang around with!" she'd accuse. And that bugged me, no end! As if I, JoJo, was perfect! I knew better.

It developed that most of the girls I did associate with had to sneak around to spend any time with me. Their parents hated me, and with obvious good reason. But all the time, instead of trying to talk things out with me or trying to figure out what was making me go wrong, Mom would just say, "It's those kids you associate with!"

It was enough to drive me up the wall, and it crossed my mind often during the lonesome hours at Juvenile Hall.

I thought of other things, too. I thought of the speed pills which had become so much a part of my life, and I longed for the time I could get back to them. It seemed to me when I took speed, I was living — and when I didn't, I was just existing, like now. I tried to block it out of my mind, and to live with what I had, but the absent thrill loomed large, and I hoped I could get back to it soon. I thought of the times in Elsinore, before I got hooked on speed — the times I'd tried sniffing glue and gasoline, the times I'd sampled just about every alcoholic mixture in existence. And through it all, I still could find no clear-cut picture of what life was all about. I was still searching, and I knew without pinning the thought down that I'd keep on searching, trying to find meaning in this mixed-up existence.

Somehow, I held together for the three months of my sentence, and it was back to court again.

The first question was to me. "Why don't you obey your parents, JoAnn?"

I shrugged. I didn't really have an answer for that. There was no point in going into all the ins and outs of it. So I squeezed out the answer I hoped they wanted. "I will — now."

Question number two was to them: "Do you think you can keep her in line this time?"

My mother nodded. "Yes, I think so."

To me: "Are you going to listen to them this time?"

"Yeah."

So it was dismissal...but on probation. I was to report to a Mrs. Crow, once a week. And Mrs. Crow, I found, was just as phony as the rest of them. She thought she had to preach me a sermon every time I went, and since the sermons were all the same, they got pretty boring, starting with the second time around.

I'd spent so much time trying to figure it all out at Juvenile Hall that I really wanted to straighten up and fly right. Or at least I thought I did. I may not have known for sure just what was right and what wasn't, but I did seriously intend to make it okay, once I was out of that place.

In the car, however, my first words to Mom were, "Hey, can I have a cigarette?" Resignedly, she pointed to her purse, and I lit up, savoring the smoke as I drew it in. I wondered if I'd enjoy the first shot of booze, the first high on speed, half as much. And I did look forward to seeing Paul again. I missed being around him far more than I missed the rest of the family. In spite of our opposite pathways, I still loved my brother.

I stayed straight for awhile. I went back to school, technically my sophomore year of high school, although I'm not sure I'd actually completed the grades before that. But it was a boring existence, and when Jenny stopped by to suggest a trip out to a ranch at Joshua Tree, I could hardly stand still, I was so eager to go. Anything to get away from home! I couldn't have cared less, at that point, that I would not again return to regular school attendance.

There was a hippie commune at Thompson's Ranch in Joshua Tree, a desert area 125 miles east of Los Angeles, and it was the kind of place I could dig. Of course it took some wine or speed to loosen me up so I could talk to people, as usual, but there was no problem getting those, so this was exciting. A couple of times, Jennie and I went there, once to stay overnight, and I felt like things were rounding into shape for me.

Then one day, Jennie dropped by again, and this time she had a new suggestion. "I'm going up to see my sister in Sacramento," she told me quietly, first making sure there weren't any other ears close by. "Like to go?"

I thought it over for a long time — probably all of ten seconds. "Sure, I'll go!" This was new, different, far-out! I had to sneak away later that afternoon, taking only the clothes on my back, but as usual I managed to cover myself with some freaky things, including a big, colorful poncho with fringes. And three of us — Jennie, a friend of hers (a fellow, but not one you'd call a boy friend), and I — were on the road with the thumbs up that same afternoon.

Our first stop of any consequence was Haight-Ashbury in San Francisco. We'd heard radio and other reports about the hippies up there, but hearing and seeing were two different things! Talk about wild. Everywhere we turned, guys walked up to us with out-and-out propositions. And even I wasn't ready for that! Hippies were all over the place, openly taking dope, smoking grass, half of them looking like maniacs. We walked through the nearby park. Guys and girls were sitting around everywhere, most of them obviously freaked out.

It didn't take long for Jennie and me to decide to move on. Both of us had bleached-out blond hair, and for some reason, that light hair seemed to turn on all the guys. For both of us, that was strictly a turn-off after the wrangles we'd had in Los Angeles, so we quickly decided to split for Sacramento.

But before we went, we ran into a guy who was a writer for the Free Press, one of the underground papers, and we became friends with him and his wife — one of those unexpected associations that just seem to happen sometimes. They were Dan and Louise Watkins, and they were nice enough to give us their telephone number, which I tucked away with a special thought in mind. At sixteen, I was still vulnerable to being picked up and questioned by the fuzz, and I figured if we got pulled over, I'd claim this couple as my parents. I was sure they wouldn't mind. They were cool.

Sure enough, just at the outside edge of San Francisco, we got collared by the cops, and taken to a nearby station. There, I asked them to call "my parents," giving them the number of our new-found friends. So they tried to call, but the line was busy, and finally, they turned us loose. We hit the road to California's state capitol.

Once there, Jennie had a problem. "I'm going with my sister," she said, "and I can't take you. But I'll find you a crash pad. I know some people up here."

Sure enough, she took me to a hippie pad, with everyone sitting around smoking grass and drinking wine, and that was the kind of scene I could dig. I was my usual withdrawn self for a time, but the wine loosened me up, and by the time Jennie split to go to her sister's, I was ready for anything.

It wasn't long before I spotted one fellow whose long hair and casual appearance were attractive, and I could see he had more than a passing interest in me, as well. He came and sat down beside me, offering me a drag on the cigarette he was smoking. I smiled and took a puff, knowing instantly this was not the tobacco I was used to. This was pure grass! I liked it.

"I'm Chuck," my crash pad neighbor said. "Chuck Sipe."

I smiled again. The wine and the marijuana made me all warm inside. "I'm Joey," I responded. "Joey Myers."

He drew lazily on the cigarette, again offering it to me. "You staying here?"

I nodded, "Just got in this afternoon. Friend of mine has a sister up here."

"I got my own mat — in there," Chuck nodded toward a nearby bedroom. "You're welcome."

Just like that. I hadn't been there an hour and a guy had picked up on me. So this was what life was all about! I was sixteen years old, and I was four hundred miles from home and I had a cool hippie with long hair who smoked marijuana and seemed to want me because I was me. I wasn't sure it was the right thing to do, but I couldn't think of anything better. So, more in desperation than happy anticipation, I gave him my answer.

"Fine!" I said. "Let's go!"

6

Communes — Psychedelic, Psychopathic

I was moved in a special way the next morning, by what Chuck Sipe said. "How about it?" He was always matter-of-fact. "You want to live with me?"

I hardly took time to give it an instant's thought. I knew I didn't love him; after all, I didn't even know him. I'd met him only the day before.

But for all of my life, I'd experienced one overriding feeling: insecurity. And Chuck Sipe, with his direct way of putting things, seemed to reflect a solidity I'd been looking for. I didn't really dig him that much, but there was certainly nothing anywhere else for me, and at sixteen, I felt it was time I found something I could cling to.

"Sure," I said. "Why not?"

He nodded soberly, then disappeared. I learned afterward that he had to give the word to another girl he'd been trying to get rid of. It was because of me, I was told, that she split. But I couldn't have cared less. I had a man to lean on and to love, and for the moment, nothing else mattered. I wasn't especially excited about our prospects, but I certainly didn't want to return home to live, and there was a certain challenge to be met in staying with Chuck. I'd been starving for love, and his acceptance of me was an open door. At that point in my life, when I saw any open door, I'd go through it!

Having left home for Sacramento with only the clothes on my back, I explained to Chuck that I really needed to return to La Puente to retrieve some of my belongings, since I'd be living with him from then on.

"No problem," he said. "I'll get George to take us down." And within an hour, we three were en route back to southern California. Chuck's friend, George, had a car, and part of the hippie crash pad philosophy was that whoever needed something someone else had, it was his. So George drove us to my parents' home.

There was no one home but Jeannette, and she just looked at me with a blank stare on her face as I went to my room, grabbed all the clothes I could carry along with some personal things, and loaded them into George's car. I also took time to raid the kitchen, knowing no generous food supply awaited us up north. To the best of my recollection, not one single word passed between us the whole time I was home, which wasn't long — probably less than half an hour. She didn't ask who Chuck was, where I was going, what was happening, nothing. And I didn't volunteer any information. Deep down, I was glad no one else was in the house. At sixteen, I was really overstepping to run off with Chuck or with anyone — as I later learned.

Then it was back to the crash pad in Sacramento, and I was glad I'd picked up some food, because there was nothing to eat except what I'd brought. That night, sharing what I'd taken at my folks' place, one of the fellows staying in the pad—a bearded, long-haired, somewhat older man named Curly — laid it on Chuck pretty thick.

"She's an evil chick. She's just not straight!" he said, after sitting and staring at me for so long I was beginning to squirm, feeling like a worm on the end of a pin. "You'd better watch out for her," he went on. "She's just out to get you!"

Chuck listened carefully, nodding his head, then twisting to study my face with cool deliberation. I turned red, and something inside me told me to bolt and run because this kind of treatment was worse than being at home. My parents had always made me think I was evil anyway, and now this open character analysis confirmed it. But I couldn't bring myself to move. I'd latched on to a new type of security with Chuck Sipe, and unless and until he decided to toss me out, I was his woman. Evil or not, I'd stay.

Chuck stared at me for a long time. This, I learned later, was his way. Chuck was a contemplator. It didn't occur to me until afterward that what he should have done was tell Curly to get lost. And when he was done scrutinizing me, Chuck said not a word.

Instead, he got up, went to the room where we'd spent the night, and came back with his guitar. Then he sat down in front of me, and plucked its strings in a plaintive non-melody that I began to realize was his own personal love-song. Evil or not, I would stay. I was his.

It took a while for me to learn something about Chuck. What I learned should have warned me, but by that time, the feeling of security he'd originally generated was such a new and heady wine that I'd have fought to keep from giving him up, if I'd had to.

He stayed high on marijuana most of the time, but I ascertained that he'd changed from the previous summer, when he'd spent the entire time freaked out on acid. He'd lived, I learned, on LSD, combined with chocolate doughnuts and chocolate milk. And as far as he was concerned, he was not an earth-dweller during that time. He was away on another planet. Now, he'd switched to grass, and being back to earth was his thing. Anyway he was my guy and we could make it together.

I began learning something new about him each day. Like the morning after we got back from La Puente. I'd picked up my make-up from home, and I was getting ready to lay it on the way I usually did when Chuck took my wrist in his hand, holding tight.

"Out!" he said, pointing with his other hand to the lipstick, eyeshadow, and rouge I had spread in front of me. "They're not natural. Everything's got to be natural."

I hesitated. For all the years since I'd been old enough to sneak into my mom's make-up, I'd doused myself good with it. Without make-up, I wasn't me. Yet, here was this man I'd attached myself to, saying it had to go. It was confusing, just like it had always been at home.

"Natural!" Chuck repeated, his eyes riveted on mine. He meant it. There was force in his voice that would not be denied.

So I threw away all the make-up, but not without an unidentified thought flitting through the corners of my mind: "Wow! He's weird!"

Not long after that, Chuck insisted I call my folks, to tell them where I was and what I was doing. "They've got a right to know!" he proclaimed righteously. "You've got to tell them you've fallen in love!"

"What?" I said. *Love* was an unknown word in my home.

Never in my life had I said, "I love you, Mom!" or "I love you, Dad!" It was unheard of. I'd even get up and leave the room when there was a song about love on the radio or TV, because I was embarrassed. But Chuck wouldn't listen.

"You call them!" he demanded. "Now!"

I had no choice. "Mom," I said when I had her on the telephone, "I've fallen in love!"

"What?" It was the familiar high-pitched scream. And then a torrent. "Where did you go? What do you know about love? Where are you, anyway?"

I was shocked. What did I know about love? Less than nothing! It was the first time I'd ever heard her use the word. She'd never mentioned it to me; she'd never said one word about the so-called facts of life, physical or otherwise. But I thought I'd better answer her other questions. "I'm in Sacramento," I told her, "and I've met this really groovy guy named Chuck, and we're in love. Oh, Mom, it's wonderful!"

Her next words came only after several seconds' delay, and I wondered if we'd been cut off. "You better get home!" she said. "Your dad's been worried about you."

That was a laugh. During all the time I could remember, my dad had never given me the slightest thought, much less worry. The world and my mom were up to their old phoniness.

"No, Mom," I said quietly. "I'm staying with Chuck. We'll stop by some time, so you can meet him." And because there was nothing more to say after I'd met Chuck's ultimatum of informing my folks, I decided to choke off the conversation. "Bye, Mom." I hung up before she could say any more.

"Way to go!" Chuck said quietly. "You're okay, Jo." It was about as near to an expression of love as I ever got from him.

It was fun, having someone to lean on, and as time went by, I came to feel more and more dependent on the man I'd chosen to share my life. Not that he changed — I found that he was downright peculiar in a lot of ways. For instance, he'd disappear into a store and keep me waiting for an hour or more at a time. It took me a long while to discover that he was doing his thing...and that his thing was looking at pornographic magazines.

Again, I knew deep down I should leave him behind and go my own way, but I couldn't make myself do it. The knowledge that he

had me available for his sexual gratification anytime he wished —
yet he preferred pictures to the real thing — was terribly
disturbing. It made me feel inadequate, but of course that was
nothing new. I'd felt inadequate from the day I was born. So I
clung to the thin thread of security that life with Chuck Sipe
provided. But I didn't like Sacramento, and I began to urge a
change of scene I was sure would be good for us both.

"Chuck," I said one night after enjoying the satisfaction of
knowing I was loved and wanted, "let's go to Joshua Tree to a
commune there. It's cool — really far out. It's just right for you and
me!"

There was a brief silence, in which I wondered if I'd guessed
wrong on Chuck's feelings about Sacramento. Then, "Why not?"
and I slept that night with the knowledge that we'd soon be on our
way to a new scene, one that I was sure would hold better things
for us both. My constant search for truth and purpose to my life, I
was sure, would now be rewarded at last.

Next morning, without announcing his intentions, Chuck left the
apartment and returned later with a large suitcase. In his usual
silent fashion, he painted it all kinds of psychedelic dayglo colors.
I'd have liked to do that myself, with my interest in art, but I knew
better — even after this brief time of living with Chuck Sipe —
than to try to move in on him when he was involved in something.
So I let him mix up the dayglo, letting drop in my mind the familiar
word that fit so many things he did: "Weird!"

We sorted out the things we wanted to keep, and crowded them
into the one big suitcase. And early next morning, we were at the
highway heading south, thumbling our way to whatever fate held
for us in southern California. There were several short rides to get
us out of Sacramento, and by mid-morning, we were stranded on a
freeway on-ramp, shivering and wondering why we'd ever started
out.

It was drizzling, but it was also freezing. After a half-hour or
more of standing there hoping for a ride, I reached up to brush
back my hair. I was shocked to feel icicles hanging from it. Chuck,
too, I saw, had ice forming in his long hair, and suddenly I couldn't
stand this any longer.

"Chuck!" I sobbed, clinging to him. "We're going to freeze to
death!"

He pushed me away so he could look at me, and I saw that his own teeth were chattering from chill. Then, his briefer-than-usual contemplation complete, his decision: "No, we're not! Come on!"

And leaving the multi-colored suitcase containing our meager possessions at the side of the on-ramp, we ran together onto the highway. If we had no other way to get to southern California, we'd run there. But at least the movement chased away some of the frightening numbness that had begun to creep over us both.

Perhaps because of the apprehension of those moments when I was sure we'd be frozen at the roadside, I have no recollection of the remainder of the trip. All I know is that we managed to find our way to La Puente and to my parents' house by early evening, after a series of rides down the state. If I'd expected to be met with open arms like the prodigal daughter I was, I was wrong. There was the usual reserve from both my parents, shared now by my sister and brother as they looked with open suspicion on the long-haired hippie I had brought back with me.

However, despite the aloofness, our presence was accepted, we were fed, and Mom laid out a separate bed for Chuck, with a place for me on the couch in another room. But Chuck was having none of that.

"Over here!" He wanted me in his bed, but I was in my parents' home, and I didn't exactly feel comfortable in that situation. I shook my head.

"Come on!" He was even more insistent. And when I hesitated, "You don't and I'll yell till your folks come in and then what'll you tell them?"

The hysterical tone in his voice made me sure Mom and Dad would be coming in any second to see what was wrong. My mind was popping with one word: "Freak!" But I felt at the same time that I had no choice. To avoid a wild scene, I got into Chuck's bed with him. I excused myself on the basis that I'd always had a submitting nature, and in this situation, I felt I had no logical way to go other than yielding to Chuck's stronger will.

The scene next morning was one I'd rather not recall. Even Dad got uptight about it — the very idea, JoJo sleeping with this hippie right in her own folks' house! Several things were said, and we ended up bundling a few of my clothes I'd left at home into a pack and walking over to Janice's house, where one of her friends

agreed to drive us to Joshua Tree that same day. I recall thinking
on the way, as I glanced at Chuck out of the corner of my eye, "I
don't want to be with him!"

But where could I go? I'd blown it — again — at home. There
was nowhere to turn. Chuck still represented the closest thing to
security I could find. Perhaps the new setting would change things
around. I could only hope so.

It was long past dark when we drove up to the front of
Thompson's Ranch, just beyond the village of Joshua Tree, but as
though they'd been expecting us, two men walked slowly out to
the car. One was Bishop John — the owner of the ranch and the
leader of the hippie cult he'd established there; he was about forty,
wearing long hair like Chuck's, but with a full beard, and wearing a
beautifully sequined robe that almost dragged the ground.

The other appeared to be an Indian — with really long, black
hair, and likewise wearing a long robe. I recalled seeing Bishop
John on my previous visits with Jennie, but this tall Indian was
someone new.

"Come in, come in!" were John's welcoming words. "Would
you like some squaw tea?"

Squaw tea, sometimes called desert tea because it's made from
plants native to the area, tasted better than anything I'd ever
sampled. Hot and pungent, it warmed and satisfied at the same
time. And so began one of the strangest periods of my life...a time
when I would change in many ways. Life in a commune is, to say
the least, different.

Bishop John, as he was known, had opened up the commune
himself, in the belief that young people should be able to do what
they wanted to, free from the conventions of society. He owned
the land at Thompson's Ranch, including the big house where he
had his own pad, along with a number of smaller back houses, and
even an outhouse or two.

It was a strange existence. No one worked, nor ever did
anything he didn't want to. We just did what we wished, enjoyed a
freedom unparalleled in the outside world. If we wanted
something, we'd get together and send out our vibes, and then sit
back and wait for the favorable results. Like when we'd decide we
wanted some peyote. We'd simply sit down together and meditate
and tell each other, "Send out your vibes!" Inevitably — whether

our message was reaching into the depths of hell to bring out Satanic assistance or what — the results would be what we were seeking. Before the day was out, a guy arrived directly from Mexico, and we had enough to last us for months. Looking back on that experience, it's scary, but we accepted it as routine at the time.

It was the same way with food. Whether they hoped to kill us with kindness or what, I don't know, but whenever we'd "send out our vibes" for food, it would invariably show up — boxes of foodstuffs, brought by townspeople who I'm sure would gladly have helped us head for parts unknown, never to darken the doors of Joshua Tree again. And if it wasn't the people from the village, it was someone from our own group, who'd managed some way or other to accumulate a stock of provisions for us.

At first, I was my usual withdrawn self there at the ranch. It had always been difficult, if not impossible, for me to open up to others — unless I could lean on wine or acid or grass or some other support. After the heavy trips I'd had on acid, I was frightened to drop again, but Chuck kept insisting.

"Come on, Joey!" he'd say. "You know — it'll help you with your hangups! Take it! Take it!" He sounded like I was a child having to take medicine. So I dropped acid with him, and as usual, things got a lot looser inside of me and outside, too. After all, everyone around me was dropping, so I'd have been out of it if I hadn't taken it.

As time went by, I lost most of the inhibitions I'd had all my life. Continuing the "natural" theme Chuck insisted on, I became strictly vegetarian, and it didn't stop there. I got to the point where, like many others, I'd walk around the commune naked, except for a leather thong with a rabbit pouch attached. It was all part of the normal scene — everyone did his or her thing, and nobody paid any attention. When I did wear clothes, it was usually just a long dress — no bra or other underthings — along with whatever beads happened to turn me on at the time.

While it was a happy-go-lucky existence, it had its serious aspects as well — strange though they were. For one thing, I developed even greater dependence on Chuck. He became, for me, my guru; I looked up to him, largely because I had no one else to look up to, I suppose. I saw in him the respected leadership I'd hungered for at home, but never found. He was serious in his attempts to help relieve me of my hangups, although he continued with the same old hangups of his own. But he was security, and I clung to him for it. I wanted the strength he had within himself, and I knew no other way to achieve it than to lean on him.

Our commune was full of characters, as might be expected. There was June, who looked — and acted — like a witch. And at the Town House, in nearby Joshua Tree, there was the Waters family, with their tiny baby named Tree Wind. Having moved there from another commune, they opened their big house to all of us to shower and clean up when we felt like it, since such facilities at the primitive ranch were non-existent.

Then there were Elaine and Tim, a drug-devoted couple that we hung around with quite a bit. Like most everyone else around us, they were flipouts. They dug being out of touch with reality, but that sort of thing scared me. I wanted to at least try to keep my feet on the ground; I wanted the reality I'd searched for all my life, so I avoided some of the things they did. Tim was so deep in the drug scene that he knew how to brew belladonna from a desert flower, and that was one thing I wouldn't touch. I'd heard it made you hallucinate to the point where little green men were all around you, and I wasn't ready for them. Knowing (now) that Tim later died from an overdose of belladonna makes me shudder. It's a wonder I didn't let them talk me into sampling that deadly potion, with probable horrendous results.

Around us, on the ranch, others were deep into the Hobbit-hole philosophy introduced in J. R. R. Tolkien's books. To them, this fantasy was totally real, just as were most other acid-induced illusions. Having dug pits or shallow caves to hide from the cops on occasion, the commune dwellers found it an easy step to call their caves Hobbit-holes. The peace-loving little half-human creatures from the Hobbit world — something like a cross between a human being and a rabbit with their furry, two-legged existence — were a natural tie-in for hippies.

Always hospitable, always delighting in a party atmosphere, always congregating in family groups — the hippies' step to becoming Hobbits seemed to turn fantasy to reality. Again, as with Chuck, only one word comes close to adequately describing their strange behavior; weird! Chuck and I were content to look on. The Hobbit philosophy didn't send us, especially since there were cops periodically stopping by for a look-see at whatever was going on.

Somewhere along the way, the constables apparently sensed that I was well under age to be living the way I was, so one Saturday morning, I looked out the window to see a familiar auto driving up to our shack.

"Oh, great!" I thought. As usual, the place was a mess. The kitchen was totally upside down; there were some crazy paintings on the walls. Our hippie existence was plainly in evidence all over our scroungy pad.

Looking like a frightened rabbit, my mother came to the door, her eyes darting furtively in every direction like she expected a troop of wild hippies to come swooping down on her. But when she saw me, she stiffened, and her mask of fright dissolved.

"JoAnn," she said, reverting to my given name so seldom used, "you're to come home with us. Now! If you don't," she paused, glancing around the unkempt room, "the cops will come get you, so you might as well come home."

I knew that arguing would only produce a screaming fit. I didn't have much stomach for that, so I thought to myself, "Well, all right, I'll go home and get a good square meal. Then I'll sneak out again!"

Chuck was out at the time, but I didn't even bother to try to let him know. I knew others in the commune would be watching, and they'd get the word to him, so I turned to Mom and surprised her. "Okay, Mom," I said quietly. "Let's go!"

It was a long ride back to La Puente, and once I set foot inside the door, I could hardly wait till I could get away. How I hated that place! But I did gorge myself on home-cooked food, not minding that privilege at all. After everyone had settled into bed, I sneaked out and headed back to my man, my pad, and my hippie existence, hitching rides until I reached my destination shortly after mid-day on Sunday. From then on, however, I did take the precaution of hiding any time I knew the cops were on the prowl. I'd been busted often enough that I didn't relish the idea of going through all that again, now that I'd been warned.

One of the philosophic themes circulating the commune at the time was the idea that God is everywhere. I guess the technical name for it is pantheism. I'd never cared particularly about where God was until then, but I did recall my time-to-time Sunday school training, and someway, it did seem more important for God to exist in that desert hideaway.

So I latched onto the idea, and I got all turned around over it. God, I thought, is you; He's me; He's the Joshua tree over there. He's the red rock I sat on yesterday; He's here, there, everywhere — everything.   It was the first of my several turn-ons to a philosophy different from what I'd known before.   In seeking enlightenment — my personal quest for the truth, whatever it might be — I'd grasp at almost anything, sincerely believing I'd at last found the answers.   But the instant of enlightenment, to my dismay, was not to come for a long time.

About this time, Dan and Louise from the underground paper in San Francisco put in an appearance. I'd written to them a few times, and I guess they wanted to see what the hippie life was really all about. They brought their three-year-old son, and together we tramped out over the desert, where I showed them the little rock altars we'd built up to help us in endless hours of meditation.

But when I enthusiastically told them that "God is everywhere!" they looked at me like I'd flipped the same way so many others had.

"Wha-a-a-t?" was Dan's drawn-out reaction.

I was surprised, because these folks were essentially straight, and I thought they'd dig my new notion.

"What do you mean — God's everywhere?" Louise asked, so I tried, without much success, to explain what it was all about. But as usual, I couldn't get the idea across, and I ended up with the thought that they could only think I was weird, so I withdrew into my shell and was glad to see them go later on. I wanted to believe God was everywhere. It made things easier, someway. I resented anyone interfering, as Dan and Louise did, in the pattern of belief I wanted to accept. My reaching, my searching, had given me something to cling to, even though it wasn't a particularly solid something. It filled a need in my life, and I didn't want it disturbed.

I thought that my parents would come for me again, but when they didn't, I periodically dropped in on them, mostly to get another decent meal. I hated it at home, as I've said, but there was an undeniable urge to hold to the tenuous ties that had bound me to my family for sixteen years. I tried to talk to them about my new-found wisdom, but it didn't get through.   Seeing my totally browned body — from running naked in the desert sun — Mom called me a "sun-worshipper" as though that were something nasty. She hadn't changed since the day I was born.

As for blond-haired, blue-eyed Paul, I had some heavy conversations with him. At thirteen and needing the security of home and family, he couldn't see why I wanted to be away.

"Why can't you just stay home?" he'd ask.

"Paul, you just don't understand," I'd reply. I knew my own outlook on our home life was totally different from his. He thought I was getting everything I should at home, while I felt otherwise — plus I'd already tasted the freedom of being out in the big, wide world on my own. But I couldn't put my feelings into words for him, so I'd just toss it off with, "This place is just a big bore to me!"

I even tried to get Paul to accompany me back to the commune, but he wanted no part of it. He'd sort of agree with me, but down deep, he was totally square, and when the time came for me to leave, he'd always be conveniently somewhere else, to avoid a showdown.

Mom, meantime, continued to be a paradox. On the one hand, she'd send me $10 a week when I was at Thompson's Ranch, knowing I was probably hungry and needed it — which, of course, was true. But at home, she'd continue to make fun of me, and would often come out with an accusation guaranteed to make me head back for the desert in a hurry.

"How come you're the only one turned out this way?" she'd say. "How come Jeannette and Paul aren't like you? Why can't you be like Jeannette?"

And then she'd throw in the clincher, before I could come unwound enough to argue with her: "Oh, I know — you're just jealous of her!" And I'd turn away in disgust, for Mom had no idea what she was doing to me with that sort of talk.

So despite my infrequent visits home, or perhaps because of them, life in the commune seemed — at the time — the only way to go. There were hungry times; there were well-fulfilled times. It was at once a weird but strangely attractive actuality, with an unseen power that was almost frightening in itself.

I'd dropped mescaline, as well as peyote and LSD, from time to time. It didn't usually bring on my hallucinations, so one afternoon when Chuck and I wandered out into the desert after dropping a tab of it, I couldn't help getting excited about the results. It was one of those unbelievable days. The sky was so blue you could see right through it to nowhere, with bursting balls of cotton clouds playing tag across the broad expanse of heaven. We were just lying there looking up, and suddenly I saw this big, big thing in the sky.

I didn't know what it was at first, so I just kept watching, and all of a sudden it was just like a curtain opening, and a monumental figure stepped out. I looked, looked away, then looked again. It was still there, and now I knew Who it was I was seeing.

His face was just popping out of heaven, and His features were just like ours, except in different dimensions. He was somehow golden, so you could see through Him. His eyes were real, much like pictures I'd seen in my younger days. I could see them moving, ever moving. One thought chased through my mind, and one thought only: "He's perfect! It's Jesus!" I didn't have to think twice. I knew! It was so beautiful.

The whole experience was just blowing my mind. I lay petrified, unable to take my eyes away from His eyes that were looking straight into mine and beyond right into my heart. I felt like I was just pinned on the ground, with a powerful force throwing me down and preventing any movement whatsoever. I tried to turn away, to move, but He just kept looking at me, and I couldn't stir. I was really scared.

Finally, exerting an effort I didn't realize I had left in me, I jerked my head to one side, conscious of an all-encompassing power drifting over me. I managed to turn sideways to Chuck, refusing to look up again. I said to him, "Man, you wouldn't believe it, Who's up there right now!" I refused to look up at the sky all the rest of that day.

In his usual slow, bored fashion, Chuck turned to me. "Who?" he asked disinterestedly.

"Jesus!" I said. "Jesus Christ!"

At first he just looked at me, and then he sort of flipped his fingers and started laughing. I couldn't see anything to laugh about. I was perfectly serious about what I'd seen. But just as suddenly as it had all begun, I was just plain little me again, and I knew my vision was gone.

But I was happy about it, for it had been totally real for me, and I wanted to share my experience with everyone else. So I insisted that Chuck go with me back to the commune, and I began telling everyone I could find, "Hey, I saw Jesus up in the sky!" But they just looked at me and turned away, like I'd been dreaming instead of seeing a vision. I couldn't understand it. It was the first time I'd really opened up and tried to talk about something unusual — and now no one would listen. No one, that is, except June — the witch — for when I excitedly told her about it, she didn't turn aside.

"Really?" she asked seriously, and I loved her for not ignoring my unique experience. "Wow! That's neat!" she added.

Surprised, I stammered, "Do — do you believe me?"

"Sure!" she said, and I could see she meant it. It really made me happy to find someone who was willing to accept my experience on the desert. From that time on, I paid more attention to June, no matter whether she was a witch or not.

Chuck, in fact, became rather deeply involved in black magic, for June had a number of books on magic. It was evident that she not only believed in black magic, but practiced it on occasion. I read some in the books myself, but for some reason, the subject didn't send me. As for the vision, I thought little about it beyond the day it happened. Something blocked the memory and its significance out of my consciousness, blinding me to it. Much later I recalled the vision's vivid impact on me and recognized its true meaning. At the time, it was only a passing fancy, soon forgotten, as life at the commune went on in its leisurely, wandering way.

I loved the Joshua trees, the delicately balanced rock formations, the penetrating silence of the monument area. It is the only place on earth, I believe, where it is so quiet you can actually hear the silence. And seeing those stately trees with their arms upraised as Joshua's must have been, I felt a oneness with nature unlike anything I'd experienced before.

Yet those feelings didn't stop me from dropping acid with Chuck, perhaps because I felt the need to keep him at my side. I sensed from his actions that he really didn't like being with me. I could tell from the personality he exhibited when he was with others that he preferred them. They were more fun. Just as when I'd lived at home, I could never tell if I had a good personality, or if he really loved me. When I'd try to talk about it, he would say, defensively, "No — I love you. No, I like you the best. You have the best personality." But I didn't believe him. So I would drop acid or do anything else he suggested; I had to cling to him, to keep him with me.

On one trip to the monument area, after dropping some acid, we built a bonfire and were sleeping outside near it when the cops came and routed us out. It was a bummer, for it looked like they'd bust us for sure. But we learned, to our surprise, that we weren't the only ones. There were quite a number of other hippies in the same area, and for some reason, they sent us on our way instead of hauling everyone in.

But that made it more important than ever that we take an action we'd talked of, but had never moved in on. I'd picked up my birth certificate on one of my trips home, and Chuck had asked around and located someone who claimed he could alter the date on it to make it appear that I was eighteen instead of seventeen (I'd just passed that birthday), so I wouldn't be picked up as a minor.

So it was done, and I felt suddenly all grown up. I was eighteen, I felt, and my own woman and Chuck Sipe's woman and everyone else could go get lost. I wouldn't have to hide from the cops any more!

It was right after Jennie visited the ranch that the world fell in on us. I loved seeing her. She was so open and outgoing, the way I wanted to be, that just having her around was a real joy. But all too soon, she departed for a commune she knew about up north, and I was lonesome again.

Chuck was the first to hit me with the news. "Hey, man! Did you hear that about the big earthquake coming up?"

I hadn't heard anything about a big earthquake. I didn't want to hear anything. I'd lived through some small shake-ups in East Los Angeles and Whittier and La Puente. I didn't relish the idea of any others, big or small. I shook my head, no.

"It's all over the radio!" Chuck said then. "It's going to be a biggie. Half of California is going to slide off into the ocean!"

I shuddered. Chuck wasn't one to kid about such things. I could see he was genuinely shook. I had a sudden insight, shared by Chuck I was sure, of the fires of hell any giant quake would shake us into.

"When?" It was the only word I could force out — a mere whisper.

He took a deep breath. "That's the problem!" he said. "No one knows just when. But we've got to get out before it hits!"

And almost as if they were specially-sent, that night a caravan of half-a-dozen or so minibuses filled with hippies descended on the commune. They, too, had heard of the impending disaster, and they — like us — weren't going to wait for it.

"Come on with us!" they urged. "We're all going to New Mexico, where we'll be safe!"

New Mexico! That seemed a world away, but I wasn't sure. "Do you think we'll be all right there?" I asked timidly. "Will the earthquake hit New Mexico, too?"

"No," came the assurance, "we'll be safe. But there's no time to waste. You'd better come with us!"

So most of our group gathered our meager things together, and we began packing ourselves into the minibuses the new hippies were driving. It was panicsville; there was genuine fear on the faces around us. Would we get away in time? Or would we, like the rest of California, slide into the all-consuming ocean when that giant quake ripped apart the very earth we were standing on?

I climbed into the crowded bus, and as I sought a place to put my things, a feminine but ominous voice challenged my presence. "You're the one!" came the terrible threat. "We're going to cook you and eat you!"

Beside me, one of the group's hippies grinned and shrugged his shoulders. "She's flipped out," he said, reaching into his shirt pocket. "Have some grass. We got a long way to go!"

7

Onjya —
Yoga, Buddhism, Nuptials

Our exodus from the commune at Joshua Tree was quickly done. Without exception — for everyone there took the threatened catastrophe seriously — we felt we were fleeing to save our lives. We imagined ourselves to be like the fleeing Israelites in Biblical times, except that our pursuing Pharaoh was the predicted earthquake that would find California sliding forever into the sea. We were living in a make-believe world, in more ways than one.

I accepted the proffered marijuana cigarette — why not? I knew Chuck would be high on it by the time we'd gone ten miles. And later, I dropped acid; it was easier to lose myself in the dream of unreality than to face the authentic fear that still dogged my footsteps. I was deathly afraid we wouldn't get to New Mexico soon enough to avoid the fate of those poor souls caught in the impending upheaval of the western coast.

On the trip, I looked back over the nine months at Joshua Tree, wondering about some of our experiences. It had been a time of maturing, in some respects. I'd grown used to Chuck Sipe, used enough to him that I didn't hestitate to fight with him on occasion, to make up with him at other times. I still couldn't have defined my real feelings for Chuck. I doubt that I really ever loved him, but I did maintain a degree of respect for him as my security blanket...my guru.

He'd led me, for example, into becoming a so-called ordained minister in the Universal Life Church. "Won't hurt you a bit," he'd proclaimed self-righteously, "and it might be a good cover some time when we need it."

There was nothing churchly about that program. All it involved was a small "licensing fee," and a certificate that designated each of us as a "minister." I recall that we celebrated the arrival of the certificates by each dropping a tab of acid, and spending the next twelve hours or so freaked out in a state of euphoria at our good fortune in having been selected to spread the gospel of the Universal Life Church, which — as we understood it — was that if you believed in God, any way you wanted to, you could be ordained as a minister. Big deal! It smelled too straight for me. Any sense of security, of having it made in a spiritual sense, was totally missing. I accepted it only because Chuck wanted me to. I was sure in my own mind that this was far from the truth I'd searched for throughout my lifetime.

Another memory that I look back upon now carries with it an uncertainty that will never be determined. Some five months after Chuck and I arrived at the commune in Joshua Tree, a bearded stranger visited us one day, received as most everyone was, with open arms. And although no one ever questioned any visitor as to his purposes or name or origin, this sharp-eyed newcomer had a standard line he'd repeat to any who would listen:

"I am the devil!" His words were escorted by a penetrating scowl, as if he were indeed searching the soul of the one to whom his remark was intended, perhaps to captivate it forever.

Was this brief visitor — he was only with us for about a day and a half, disappearing into the nowhere from whence he came — just possibly the man whose name would later become synonymous with violent death? Was he, indeed, Charles Manson? Or was our visitor just another of the self-styled weirdos who sprung from the era of the sixties? I shall always wonder if that was an early crossing of paths portending our later association with the Manson family. The record shows that Charlie was loose at that time.

There was a brief shout of triumph as our V-W bus rolled across the Colorado River bridge separating the states of California and Arizona. Somehow, it seemed as if that river also marked the borderline of the looming calamity. We were, if not entirely safe from it, at least well on our way toward the security we sought.

I thought back, then, to the rituals that had been so much a part of our communal life at Joshua Tree. To me, these practices had represented a sense of security, of well-being. We would sit and join hands and chant our universal syllable that was supposed to attune us with God and the universe around us.

"Ohmmm!" we would chant. And again and again, "Ohmmm! Ohmmm!" Like sending out our vibes when we wanted food or drugs, our frequent intonations were a part of life, and at the time, seemed to bring a needed sense of the reality of our existence. I thought about it now, in the haze of the marijuana smoke as we rode, and I wondered what life's purpose really was. I was totally unaware, of course, of the absence of the real security of God's love. This was something that was yet to enter my life.

It was hours later, just before we reached Flagstaff in the mountainous terrain of north central Arizona, that a dread sound penetrated the smoke-filled haze of our bus.

"Hey, stash the stuff!" came a quick command from up front. "Fuzz on our tail!" The whining sirens dug into my fogged consciousness, and I looked around to see where Chuck had secluded himself, giving secret thanks for the forged date on my birth certificate.

A handsome young patrolman in a smart uniform spoke to our driver. "We'd like to talk with you folks awhile," he said, friendly enough. "Would you please follow us into Flag'? Appreciate it."

We had no choice. "They're behind us and out in front, too," our driver announced. "It's a bust!"

So? So what? I thought. *I've been busted before by better than them.*

Quietly, polite enough, they rounded us all into a big room at the patrol station, inviting us to sit down like it was a church service or something.

"Just like to rap awhile," one of the younger patrolmen said. "Where you folks heading?"

"Aimin' for New Mexico." There was quite a contrast between the long-haired, sloppy-dressed, and bearded man who replied, and the jaunty, clean-shaven young officer. "Didn't want to get caught in the California crack-up."

So our self-appointed leader proceeded to explain why we were in flight. The guards around us listened and nodded from time to time. If they failed to see any logic in our flight, they didn't say so.

"All right," the officer conceded finally. "Other than getting away from that — whatever it is that's coming — otherwise, what's your bag?"

Our leader shrugged. "Live and let live," he said slowly.

"Fine — far as it goes!" agreed the patrolman. "But what about the future? Where are you headed? What are you gonna do ten years from now?" He wasn't addressing just the man who'd answered his first question. He was asking all of us the same question.

The leader shrugged again. "Tomorrow takes care of itself," he said. "Why hassle it?"

"Grass...acid...God knows what else," our host said then. "We know you're on it. What does it really get you?" Again, he was addressing all of us, asking us to do some soul-searching I'm not sure we were ready for. Certainly I wasn't; anyone straight, like the cop, could not reason with me, for I automatically rejected whatever he proposed.

"We just want to do our thing," our guy tried to explain. "No harm to anyone who doesn't dig it."

Amazingly, the conversation went on in the same vein for another thirty minutes. We weren't being busted, not even being hassled. We were just passing the time of day with these patrolmen, who seemed bent on finding out what made us tick. It was a really strange trip, just sitting there, rapping with these guys. Some of us, and I'm afraid I was one of them, cried a few bitter tears before it was over. It was like being put through a wringer, like being forced to sit back and take a long look at ourselves. And I wasn't really ready for such a look. All I wanted was to run from reality — a day-by-day existence with no thought beyond the immediate need for protection from the impending disaster of earthquake or whatever else fate held. We feared death, because we feared facing eternal hell, but we were content to run from it rather than face the necessity for renouncing an improper way of life.

One girl who'd arrived with the hippie caravan — she couldn't have been older than sixteen, and obviously was several months pregnant — really flipped. "I wanta call my mom!" she sobbed.

They took her to the phone. Next to me, one of the older women whispered coarsely, "Cop-out!" I nodded. I figured the next thing would be loading the youngster on a bus and sending her back to mother. But surprisingly, after she'd made her call, she seemed content, sitting quietly while our captors continued their questioning.

"What you're saying," our group leader finally replied to one of the uniformed men, "is that we're not going to make it. Well, the way we feel is just the other way around." He paused, to make his point more emphatic. "We don't think *you're* going to make it!"

That seemed to bring the entire episode to its curtain time. The officer shrugged, then grinned. "Could be you're right," he said. Then, with a glance at his associates, "You're free to go, anytime."

I wanted to jump and run before they changed their minds, but I watched the leader and sat still while he slowly acknowledged our liberty. "That's cool," he said quietly. "Okay, everybody. Let's roll!"

And roll we did, on across Arizona and into New Mexico. But the pressure was off now. We'd vacated California before it slid into the ocean, and we'd survived a probable bust. Life was good. It was as if we were fulfilling our destiny. So we'd stop at night and build ourselves a big bonfire and sit around it and rap and smoke pot and sleep under the stars.

I learned that our traveling partners were deep into yoga and meditation and the law of karma, based on Buddhistic philosophy — that whatever you do in this life will come back to you in the next life, and whatever is happening to you now is the result of your last previous life. *Wow*, I thought, *I must have been really something else in my last life!* Reincarnation became, to me, a reality, and I began to worry day and night about what was in store for me. I could readily recognize that if I had to keep getting reborn again until I became perfect, I really had a long way to go.

By the time we reached our destination — a commune established in an old Indian burial ground in Placitas, northeast of Albuquerque and southwest of Santa Fe — I had listened to enough of this philosophy to really turn on to it. The group had a lot of books on yoga, and I dug in on them, as did Chuck. Here again, I was sure I was only a scant shadow away from the finality of life's truths that I'd been searching for. The possibility that I'd bridge the gap at last kept me hyped up. I just knew I was one breath away from revelations of life's realities. But of course this was not yet to be.

There were two large houses and several smaller units in our compound — some of them shacks, some actual tepees. Chuck and I took over one of the two-room shacks. When we arrived, a guy was leaving.

"Take my house!" he said generously. Some house! It was not only barren, it was a wreck! The first time it rained, the top caved in on our bedroom, and we were completely flooded out. It would be stretching a point to say it was a roof over our heads.

Placitas, we found, was an old town, and its age showed in its run-down condition. Mostly there were Indians in the area, plus a scattering of hippies like us, and a few well-established residents whose roots had been sunk deep in previous generations.

But it was not a bad existence, overall. We could get food stamps to cover our nutritional needs, strictly vegetarian. More important to us were the yoga exercises we learned, more than a hundred of them. There was a big, thick blue book listing all the exercises and meditations, and our days were spent, for the most part, in learning this new way of life.

And that wasn't the only book. There were others, generally occult, and in my thirst for knowledge of what the world around me and what I myself were all about, I read everything I could get my hands on.

For the first few months, I sent no word to my parents of my whereabouts. I was determined, at this point, to make it on my own, and I hoped the new philosophy would help me make it. There were disturbing experiences that made me want never to be in contact with my mother again. When I'd get stoned on pot, I'd get uptight, and I'd start screaming at Chuck exactly like my mom screamed at my dad. I hated myself for it, but I couldn't control it. And Chuck, like Dad used to do with Mom, would get me down on the ground and beat on me to stop the screams. I know the others around us must have heard, but theirs was a program of "do your own thing" and if that was our thing, so be it.

Only when we were high on acid did we avoid the fighting, because we had to stay on our toes to keep everything together on those LSD trips. I became aware that drugs were not acceptable to the Buddist philosophy. While I did eventually quit smoking — for a time — I couldn't let go entirely of the acid, mainly because it was easier to go along with Chuck than to battle him over such matters.

We ate mostly raw vegetables and brown rice. Not that eating or what we ate was important. The only thing that meant anything to me was the constant search for enlightenment, and if the Buddhism into which I became engulfed called for that diet, well and good. Somehow, the more I got into the study of this new philosophy and its call for total concentration to the point where the mind is dissolved and self-illumination results, the more confused I became.

The enlightenment I sought came no nearer, even though that search was a 24-hour-a-day obsession with me. I would lie in bed at night, sometimes all night long, my mind churning with fear that I would not reach the perfection I needed...that I would die before reaching the level necessary so I could be born again. It was frightening!

I would never admit it to myself, but I made no progress at all toward my goal of better understanding of myself and what life was all about. Enlightenment was a butterfly that I chased endlessly, only to find it constantly just out of my reach. And I got down on myself, the way I'd been most of my life. Others, I imagined, could find the clarification of life that was just beyond my fingertips...but never JoJo.

Chuck, whose preoccupation with his marijuana habit kept him from worrying about life and what it was all about, decided after we'd been in Placitas awhile, that it was time to change his name.

"Nature's what it's all about!" he proclaimed one evening when we were having a last drag on the ever-present pot. "So from now on, JoJo, you can call me by my new name. From now on I'm Erutan."

"Air-oo'what? What are you talking about?"

"Erutan — that's my name. From now on."

I still didn't quite get it. "Spell it," I demanded.

But instead of telling me, he found a piece of paper and a stub of pencil and carefully printed out a word: N—A—T—U—R—E.

"Now," he said, "start with the E and spell it backwards." He handed me the paper, and I did as he said: E-R-U-T-A-N.

I looked at it and grinned. "Hey, that's neat!" I exclaimed. Then, not to be outdone, "Okay," I said. "You're Erutan. And from now on, my name's going to be different, too. From now on, I'm Onjya."

And I carefully printed it out on the paper. O-N-J-Y-A.

"Crazy name," Chuck — Erutan, that is — announced. "What's it mean?"

I'd thought about it before, but hadn't ever followed it up, and now was a good time to do it. "It's JoAnn in Russian," I said. "I never did like JoAnn, but I dig Onjya. Lots better than JoJo or Joey."

"Dig!" said my partner. "Because your mom's parents were Russian — right?"

"Right on!" I replied, adding just for effect, "Erutan."

He smiled and reached for me. There were times when our communication was real, when we were in tune with each other, when with or without being high on pot or acid or speed or whatever, we were on the same wave length, and life was good.

I hadn't written to Mom, as I explained previously, because I hated myself for being so much like her and having those screaming fits that disrupted everything so thoroughly. But by the time we'd been in New Mexico for five months or so, both Erutan (I still thought of him as Chuck most of the time) and I were becoming restless. The commune was constantly beset by weirdos of one sort or another. Anything we'd managed to acquire in the way of worldly goods was often as not ripped off by these nomads who came and went almost on a daily basis.

"I think we ought to split ourselves," I told Erutan one day, and not wanting to admit I was actually homesick, "Maybe there isn't really going to be an earthquake in California. It was supposed to happen a long time ago."

In his usual deliberate fashion, Erutan thought it over. "You're right, Onjya," he said seriously. Then, a surprise idea from him: "Maybe we wouldn't get hassled so much if we — made it legal."

I didn't care either way, but I could see the logic in his reasoning. "Okay," I said. And then with a grin, I added, "If you want to be an old married man, that is."

"Don't matter to me," he admitted. "But if we've got a license and all that, they can't question your age or anything."

"Let's do it!" I said.

But it wasn't all that easy, we found out. Because I was only eighteen, according to my birth certificate, I had to obtain permission from a parent before the New Mexico authorities

would issue the license. I finally wrote to my mom, telling her
where we were, and asking for a written statement authorizing me
to be married with her permission. She sent it right back, and the
way was open, except that there was a marriage license fee to be
paid. Mom hadn't bothered to enclose any cash along with her
permission statement, and cash was something we didn't have.

Erutan solved that problem within a couple of days. Quietly,
and without telling me till later, he "borrowed" the money and
some extra, too, from a guy who'd stopped at the commune
briefly. We got the license, and a fellow-minister in the Universal
Life Church — a long-haired, bearded hippie-type who lived in
the town of Placitas with his wife and kids — agreed to perform an
East Indian ceremony for us.

It was the social event of the season for the commune, but
different in many ways from the average wedding "outside" in the
normal world. There really wasn't much planning. I wore just a
plain everyday dress — in fact, the only one I owned. Erutan wore
what he had on — jeans and a patched shirt. It was about mid-day,
and we moved down beside a stream that ran past one side of the
commune area. There were maybe twenty-five people from the
commune gathered around us.

We were all in a circle, and a little girl from the group came up to
me with a bunch of tiny wild flowers she'd gathered from the
desert nearby.

"Here," she said with a bashful smile, "these are for you." I
accepted them, smelled their pungent desert scent, and reached
out to touch the child's golden hair — my unspoken thanks for her
generous gesture. It was the most precious moment of the entire
ceremony!

Then everyone but the minister and Erutan and I sat down, and
he read from Kahlil Gilbran's *The Prophet*, all about love and
being one and things like that. I couldn't get very excited about it.

The next step was for everyone there to become "water brothers
and sisters," made possible by passing a water jug around the
circle, with everyone taking a hit off of it. Then we passed around
a pipe packed with pot, and we all took a hit off of that. After a few
more words of his own — and I must admit that I haven't the
vaguest memory of what they were — the minister said the
traditional, "I now pronounce you man and wife," and it was done.

Erutan placed on my finger an old Moroccan Buddhist ring that he'd picked up in a head shop or thrift shop somewhere and had worn for a long time himself.

"See, now you guys are married!" said the minister, looking serious at me when we went to sign the papers afterward. I was thinking, "Oh, big deal!" He seemed kind of straight to me, and I couldn't dig that sort of attitude.

Then it was feast time, as we all went back to the main house. Someone in the bunch had made a big batch of grass cookies, liberally laced with marijuana, so that if we didn't get stoned by smoking it, we'd still absorb plenty through eating it. And as the afternoon wore on, everyone drifted off in a marijuana fog to do their own thing.

There was no honeymoon, no rejoicing, no nothing. I was Mrs. Charles Edward (Erutan) Sipe, it was true, but there was no use pretending. I wasn't happy, married or unmarried. I didn't love the man who was now my husband. Maybe I was protected from the authorities, maybe the little piece of paper did that for me, but it stopped there.

And it didn't help when late that afternoon, without knocking, the guy who'd stopped by the commune stamped through the door to confront my spouse. "All right!" he yelled. "Gim'me my money!"

Erutan, thoroughly stoned at this point, looked pained as he carefully surveyed our visitor. "I don't have it!" he said innocently.

"The hell you don't!" the guy accused. "You're the one lifted it. You can't rip me off like that!"

Erutan held up a restraining hand. "Peace, brother!" he said. "Have some grass." And he extended a marijuana cigarette.

Without a word, but still scowling, the guy turned and stormed out the door. When he was gone, Erutan turned to me.

"Get our stuff packed, man," he said quietly. "We got to split — quick!"

8

Exodus — From There to Where?

I wasn't unhappy about leaving Placitas, so I welcomed my husband's words. "I'll be ready in half-an-hour!" I told him.

Gathering our meager belongings together, I thought about some of the reasons I was so glad to be going. The whole atmosphere of the place was degenerate. Despite our own questionable character, those around us were, I felt, even worse.

Take the babies in the commune: they were simply turned loose, wandering around without supervision, subject to whatever care anyone besides their mothers chose to give them. The girls who'd brought them into the world were, like us, high on pot or dope most of the time, ignoring their little ones. I'd cleaned and fed some of them myself on several occasions.

Then there were the two characters who lived in the broken down trailer in front of our shack. They were alcoholics — constantly drunk — and I frequently shook them down for money and anything else they had that we could use. It didn't take much effort; they were usually so far gone they'd give us anything we asked, if they had it.

And so I was glad to see the last of the place. By the time I was ready to go, darkness had settled over the commune, so it was no trouble at all to quietly walk away from the place. Once again, we stood at the side of the road, patiently awaiting the ride we knew would be offered, sooner or later. The fact that we were over 800 miles from our destination, California, didn't cross our minds.

Placitas being somewhat off the beaten track, we stood and waited a long time before a motorist finally slowed. We ran to jump into his noisy car. Young, about Erutan's age, our driver seemed to sense our urgency to get away.

"She makes a lot of noise," he said of his auto, "but she'll get us to Albuquerque, far as I'm going. Where you headed?"

"That'll be fine," Erutan told him. "Think we'll head on west from there."

He dropped us off at Highway 66, and we took up our early morning vigil for the ride that would move us further toward California. "Ain't likely to catch up with us now!" I heard my husband mutter.

"Did you really have that guy's money? Was that how you bought the license?" I asked.

He nodded, drawing on his grass cigarette. "He didn't need it," he explained. "He was loaded."

I couldn't help being curious. "How much?" I asked.

"Just a hundred," Erutan said. "Should have grabbed more."

A quick thought flitted through my mind. There must be at least seventy-five dollars left. Maybe we should use it for a couple of bus tickets and travel to California in style. But I was afraid to mention it. Why pay cash for something you could get for free? I knew that would be my husband's answer. That much cash would buy a lot of pot, much more important than any comfort we might have in traveling.

The series of rides we accepted to get us back to California included another unpleasant experience with a truck driver, with my husband sitting silently by while I suffered indignities not fit to be recounted here. I'd gladly have jumped from the roaring truck to whatever horrible death I might have faced, but there was simply no way I could get out. I made up my mind, though: if something like that ever happened again, I'd kill myself.

Our unannounced arrival at my parents' home in La Puente at mid-morning a couple of days later was not exactly a joyful event. Dad had already gone to work. Paul was in school, and when Mom came to the door to see us standing there with our gear, she had a typical reaction.

"What are you doing here?"

It was as though she'd hoped never to see us again.

"We're married!" It was the first thing I could think of to justify our return. "Everything's all right, Mom!"

And so began a less than pleasant stopover in the one place I'd sworn I'd never return to. The atmosphere in which I'd grown up, tense at best, was now more taut than ever. All we could do was attempt to ignore the evidences of inhospitality as if they did not exist. After all, there was a roof over our heads, there was food to eat, and such as it was, there was companionship, even though all were grudgingly shared.

Erutan made feeble efforts to find work, but mostly he was just faking it. We kept on with the one thing productive that we'd learned in our earlier travels — making beaded leather goods and selling them as tote bags, dope pouches and the like; we also carved pipes, handy for marijuana smoking. And I pursued a long-time inclination to make flutes from bamboo and other wood, and to play them.

We tried to sell our goods in Hollywood, but we weren't properly organized to get the job done, so it was a washout. But we ran into old friend Jennie on the streets there, and that was a good scene.

We'd left the house that morning on less than good terms. In fact, for the first and only time, Dad laid a hand on my husband.

"I come home tonight, I expect you to have yourself a job!" Dad stormed into our room to rouse us before he went to work — something he'd never done before.

Erutan rubbed at his sleepy eyes. "Hey, like cool it, man!" he said.

"Tired of all this nonsense!" Dad seemed to be muttering to himself. Then, without another word, he swung at Erutan's face, a sort of half-hearted slap with the back of his hand rather than an out-and-out punch. There was plenty of beard to soften the already-light blow, so I'm sure Erutan hardly felt it. And Dad, as though ashamed of what he'd done, turned and stalked out.

"Forget him!" I said to my husband. "He won't do anything more."

So finding Jennie was like coming home again. She was with a new boy friend, and didn't have time to talk then, but the future outlook was good.

"I'll see you tonight!" she promised. And she not only came over, she helped us with our beadwork for the next several days.

There came a day when four of us were headed for the beach — Jennie, her friend Rod, Erutan and I. I was coming down off speed at the time, and it was getting to me a little. I was pretty nervous, so I didn't especially like the idea of thumbing our way.

"Hey, come on!" Jennie told me. "Nothing's going to happen. Get hold of yourself, Jo."

"Onjya," I reminded her. I'd checked her out on our new names the first thing, of course.

"Yeah, Onjya, but you're still Jo to me."

About that time a car rolled to a stop — just one guy in it, four of us, couldn't anything happen, could there? We got in — Jennie and Rod in front, Erutan and I in the back, and we began to roll. I leaned back and closed my eyes, and was almost immediately half-asleep.

Then I began picking up on what the guy who'd stopped for us was saying. It was weird. "Hey, you got any grass? Better yet, how about some acid. I can dig it."

My husband passed a marijuana cigarette up to him. "Thanks, man!" He drove silently for a time, then through my own half-fog, I heard snatches of a frightening conversation.

"Ran right in front...smacked him good...man, you should've seen the blood squirtin' out...it was groovy!" I learned later, from Jennie, that he'd been describing running over a little boy.

I opened my eyes, and what I saw then, I couldn't take. Our driver had pulled a pistol from his pocket, and was holding it up for the others to see. Memories of other rides at other times washed over me, and I freaked out. This was too much.

Without a word, I pulled at the door handle on my side, pushed the door open, and jumped out. The road came up and smacked me, hard. I hadn't thought what it would be like. I hadn't thought anything — except getting out of that car. I rolled over and over, and I could feel the rough surface tearing at my skin. The instant I lit, a shocking pain ripped into my right ankle, but there were so many other hurts at the same time, I didn't think anything about it.

Half-conscious, I could see out of the corners of my eyes that our driver had pulled to the side of the road ahead of us, that other drivers were likewise stopping. He would now come after me with the gun. I knew it!

I got up to run, but my right foot refused to work. I hopped over to the nearest car and banged on the window.

"Help me!" I screamed. "He's got a gun!"

The frightened driver took one look at me and scooted off. I hopped to another car. Same result. I began to cry.

Then, out of a small truck that had stopped, came a young man about my husband's age. He walked up and took my right arm. "Here," he said, "let me help you. You may have broken your leg!"

For the first time, I thought about the pain in my right foot. And I thought about truck drivers, too. Maybe they weren't all bad, after all.

"Thanks," I murmured, and let him help me to the side of the road. Then I looked up, and here came Erutan, Jennie, and the others, including the driver of the car I'd jumped out of.

"Hey, man, why did you jump out?" My husband wore a strange look, like he thought I'd flipped or something.

"What do you mean — why did I jump out?" I snapped back. "I probably saved you guys' lives!"

The car driver who'd come along with them looked at me curiously, then spun on his heels and ran to his car and split. "Get his license number!" I screamed. "He's got a gun!"

The next thing I knew, I was in a hospital and three cops were shooting questions at me. I tried to answer the best I could, but somehow, I couldn't get it together. The pain from my ankle was really getting to me now.

But I was conscious enough to know what they said when they walked out. "Freaked out on LSD," one of them said.

"Yeah, that's why she jumped," another put in. "They do weird things when they're on that stuff."

I wanted to call them back and tell what really had happened, but I just couldn't do it. Let them think what they wanted. Then I got some more bad news.

"They won't do anything about your leg at this hospital," my husband said. "Have to take you to Kaiser. I called your mom."

So it was wait for Mom to come bail me out once again, and then the long drive to the Kaiser Hospital in the Hollywood area of Los Angeles. I screamed when the doctor there first touched my ankle.

"Sorry about that," he said quietly. "Looks like you've got a badly busted up ankle, Mrs. Sipe. There's nothing in the world more painful than that." He looked at me soberly. "We'll have to get some X-rays, then we'll see what we can do."

Each time anyone touched it, I'd scream out in pain at the top of my lungs. Then, before he attempted to set it, came a merciful hypo. When I woke up, I had a white cast on my right leg from just below the knee to clear around my foot. There was still some general pain, but nothing like what it had been before.

"You sure pulled a good one that time, young lady!" My mom could always come up with something to make me feel just great.

Once I got out of the hospital and back home again, I put the pressure on my husband. "Let's split!" I urged. "I can't stand it here much longer."

He looked at me in that direct way of his, letting my message soak in. Then, "Okay," he said. "Soon as we can get away without a big scene."

It wasn't easy, adjusting to the crutches I had to use, but they did lead to catching rides easier. Only a few days after we'd settled in at home after two days in the hospital, we were on our way to Laguna Beach.

"Good place to make out," Erutan said, and I knew he was referring to the marijuana and harder drug traffic.

So we sold our beaded bags and our pipes and lived a precarious existence there for a time. But the vibes were bad; Erutan was surly, so was I. The awkward cast on my leg didn't help. We were sharing a pad with a group of other hippies, but they didn't dig us, and the feeling was mutual. I dropped acid again, hoping to lose myself in its illusions, but nothing came of it. I just remained miserable.

Finally, Erutan came up with a hoped-for solution. "Good gig going on in Seattle," he told me. "You game?"

I guess he was referring to my leg. Could I stand another session on the road? I didn't bother to think about it. Anything was better than this miserable existence.

"Let's go!" I said. We were on the road an hour later. My leg was hurting, but I'd stashed away some speed pills before we'd decided to leave, and as long as I had them, I didn't really care whether we were thumbing or riding. It was all the same and it was all good because we were getting away from a bad scene.

I don't recall anything about the trip to Seattle, probably

because there were, thankfully, no more problems like I'd had with the Los Angeles-bound truck driver. Somehow, after a series of day-and-night rides in which I slept away much of the time in the cars of the people who picked us up, we got there.

I'd learned long before that Erutan's mother was a Seattle resident, and from hints he'd dropped, I had a hunch I knew something of what kind of person to expect. She was an elementary school teacher, I knew, but according to her son, she didn't mind an occasional pull on the weed. That enlightened attitude, I figured, couldn't be as bad as the super-square existence my own parents favored.

I was wrong. From the minute we arrived, things were less than upbeat. "Where'd you find her?" Those were the first words we heard from my mother-in-law. Then, to me "Sonya, did you say your name was?"

"Onjya," I corrected her, trying to smile. "It's the Russian name for JoAnn."

"You Russian?" And before I could confirm my heritage, she went on. "Never did trust the Russians!"

We hadn't been there an hour before Erutan was off in a corner by himself looking at a sexy magazine he'd picked up. For some reason, this bugged me.

"You on that again?" I gasped. "What's the matter with you?"

And without waiting to find out what had triggered my own outburst, my husband's mother jumped on me. "Let the poor boy alone!" she challenged. "No wonder he's had his problems!"

All my fault, of course. Deep down, I wasn't sure but what it was. Otherwise, why should Erutan come up with such actions? It didn't occur to me that maybe he had some crazy hangup about his own father, who — I understood — was divorced from his mother, and lived somewhere nearby in the Seattle area.

But rough as it was, we settled in at my mother-in-law's place, soon discovering that she was deeply involved with a local disc jockey, and that like us, they didn't hesitate to drop LSD or to get stoned on pot at every opportunity.

Erutan and I found a ready market for our wares — the beaded bags, the pipes, and other hand-crafted articles. Love-ins in Seattle parks were a familiar scene, and it was easy to peddle our production.

We frequently found ourselves in the head shop section of the city where hippies were all over the place. It was here that we ran into Elaine, with whom we'd shared pot and LSD at Joshua Tree. Her husband, Tim, who'd tried to turn me on with belladonna, had died from an overdose of that very drug, and now Elaine was with her parents in Seattle.

"It was a bad scene!" That was all she'd say about it, and I recalled my own dread of the poisonous effects of the desert weed.

The constant bickering with Erutan's mother finally got to us both, so we moved out, taking a place in a converted garage, behind a house where a dope dealer lived. He had a machine for turning out bronze hashish pipes, and both my husband and I took a hand in helping produce them. This was our kind of thing!

We'd go to the love-ins or the rock concerts in the park, display our pipes laid out on a blanket, and sell them for whatever price we could. Of course part of the selling technique involved demonstration, so we'd be smoking the hash ourselves — stoned to oblivion — long before the day's event was over. The hash, a strong residue from grass, was heavy. It was a groove. We dug it.

But I also dug something else in Seattle. I was on the street near a head shop one day when a group of dancing, chanting young people caught my eye and ear. When the dance was over, one of them handed me a tract, and I looked to see what might be the source of their energetic performance. They seemed so serene, so content. Maybe this was for me!

It was, I found, about Hare Krishna, a sect I'd heard about but had never chanced to run across before. Krishna, I learned, had come from the planet Lotus Flower, and he played the flute — like me. That was the convincer. Without hesitation, I went to the nearby Krishna temple, hoping my search for inner peace had finally ended.

I began to attend the temple once a week, and I practiced a personal philosophy combining bits of all the religious currents I'd encountered...Buddhism, Universal Life Church, a childhood smattering of Christianity, and the exciting Hare Krishna chants. Once more, I was sure I'd shortly gain the full enlightenment of life's secrets. This had to be it, if only I could turn the final corner.

But as it turned me on, it turned Erutan off. He began to resent my frequent chanting, the exercises I did, the spicy foods I began to produce in conformity to my new-found cult. And his disenchantment with my own fascination only served to make me dig deeper into the faith. In reality, my interest in Hare Krishna was two-fold: I was, of course, looking for the elusive truth, and I hoped this at last might be it; further, I discovered that the sect had an active kitchen which provided unlimited food for its adherents. It was easy to project religious involvement to satisfy the interests of an empty stomach.

The more I pursued Hare Krishna, the more I was convinced that my life with my husband was evil, a sin of the first order. I was debating whether to leave him, to give my whole life over to my new-found philosophy. Life, in fact, became a continuing dream, a neat escape from reality as I envisioned the freedom I would enjoy being totally wrapped into the Hare Krishna concept.

I read in one of the books offered me that the only way to be free was to become unattached from everything. That meant, of course, from my husband, and I had tremendous guilt feelings for my association with him, uncertain as it was. My marriage was sinful. Everything that others saw as moral or normal was likewise charged with evil. The inner peace I'd sought changed to prickling turmoil. But I lacked the final conviction needed to walk away from my husband. I could not bring myself to commit my whole life to the Hare Krishna movement, the way others did. The fulfillment they appeared to enjoy escaped me. I retained interest, always hoping, but there remained the old emptiness I'd tried so long to satisfy. Then, still representing a strange sense of security for me, Erutan slacked off on his own activities of pushing dope and selling underground papers, and gave me the word.

"It's your turn, man!" he said to me. "I been bringing in the bread ever since we got here. Now that you've got that stinking cast off your leg, you got to come through, man. You got to go over to Tacoma tomorrow. I've got you all set up."

True, after more than three months of wearing it, I had just had my leg cast removed by a Seattle doctor. My right leg, encased for so long, was again beginning to bear a natural look, instead of the chalky, shriveled, shapeless mess it had become. I'd been able to walk on it, of course, but I was happy to be free of such an unpleasant burden.

I looked at my husband, wondering what scheme he'd come up with this time. "What's in Tacoma?" I asked suspiciously.

Without answering, he picked up a copy of the underground paper he'd been peddling, pointing to a classified ad in it.

"Wanted: attractive girls for pleasant, exciting work. Make fabulous money, only few hours a day. Call Mr. Smith..." and it gave a telephone number.

I didn't waste words. "Whorehouse?" I asked.

Erutan looked hurt. "No way!" he said. "I called and checked it out. It's," and he paused, apparently almost reluctant to fill me in on the details, probably because he knew how I would react, "it's body-painting. All you got to do..."

"Forget it!" I burst out. "Nobody's going to smear paint all over me!"

"Now wait a minute," my husband said. "It ain't that bad!"

He went on to explain that all I'd have to do was answer the phone and convince the caller that doing his thing with paint on an attractive nude body would give him kicks. There wouldn't be anything beyond that.

I shivered, recalling truck drivers who'd gotten their kicks without benefit of paint. But I knew, deep inside, that I wasn't strong enough to resist my husband, once his mind was made up.

"What's the score on the bread?" I asked.

"Great!" he said. "Ten bucks for just fifteen minutes." He paused, knowing what came next wouldn't send me very far. "You get half."

I stared at him. "Who gets the other half?" I asked. If it stayed in the family, if it came to him, maybe...

"The guy who runs the studio," he explained casually. "After all, he's got the action."

I ended up taking a bus for the long ride to Tacoma the next morning. The place was small, half-dark, stale. The guy who owned it was oily.

"Hey, you're fine!" he said after I'd stripped. "You'll be great. Now, here's how it works." And he had me listen while another girl, wearing only the briefest of panties, gave the come-on to a caller. Patrons could have their choice — body-painting or photo-taking, using their own cameras, of course. The idea was to convince them on the phone that they'd get their money's worth.

I wasn't very convincing. I made ten dollars my first day. The men who came were, of course, perverts, and no customer, no pay. I hated Erutan for setting me up for this monstrous misadventure. I tried to seek solace in the newfound religious sanctuary of my mind. It didn't help. I was ashamed, unhappy, hurt. And yet, largely because my husband demanded it, I returned the next day and the day after that. For two weeks, I kept the routine, but by the end of that time, I was so depressed that even burying myself in pills or pot didn't help.

"I've had it!" I screamed at Erutan when I got home one night. "I'm never going back!"

Typically, he just looked at me for a moment, then extended a marijuana cigarette. "Peace, man," he said to me. "I need you to help me tomorrow, anyway. Big pop festival — Ike and Tina Turner — we ought to make a killing!"

Killing...I liked the word. I felt like killing. The men who called and came with evil intent...my mixed-up far-out husband... myself. Killing. I drew deep on the pot. If I had to go back to that Tacoma dive, there'd be a killing for sure. The only question was, which one?

9

Pot Pushing, Pregnancy —
The Manson Family

I didn't have to go back. Apparently satisfied that I'd tried to do my part, my husband was content to have me help him push the dope at the pop festivals that were very much a part of the Seattle scene that autumn of 1969.

Nor did he mind my own exhibitionism, largely induced by my being loaded on whatever we happened to be pushing at the time. I wore only a leather loin cloth, going openly topless and sometimes feeling offended because what I considered to be "dirty old men" were leering at me. At other times, I'd wear a sheer slip, without a bra, of course, and that seemed to attract even more attention than when I went topless.

It helped our sales, of course; there were thousands of people milling around, and we moved a lot of pipes, with the hash to go in them. With both of us stoned, it's a wonder we were able to make sense out of the necessary business transactions, but that never seemed to bother us.

We had Erutan's mother on our side, too. She'd come to our place or to wherever we were pushing the stuff, and she went right along with us. Getting other drugs was no problem; we were "in" as far as the hippies were concerned, because we dared to be as "far out" as anyone. The result was getting all the drugs we could handle, just for the asking. Personally, I preferred getting drunk on wine, but my husband didn't dig that, so it was usually grass, hash, speed, or whatever other drugs were favored at the time. One thing about it — when we were stoned, we had no worries about anything else. So staying stoned was our thing. Other troubles simply faded away as we smothered them with whatever was available, short of smack — the big H.

Yet, through it all, I continued seeking, always seeking. Where's the truth? What is it? How do I learn it? It bugged me, and I bugged my husband about it, but that didn't help. The elusive truth, whatever and wherever it was, remained cloaked in secrecy, no matter how hard I tried to find it through the various cults and faiths I'd encountered.

I could have — in fact, I should have — worried about what drugs could do to me, both mentally and physically. I didn't. They were just a part of the eternal search, and I looked to them as a possible key to unlock the door of the unrevealed reality I sought. Obviously this key was a total misfit, but I failed to realize how misguided I was, and I stayed with the drug scene with no thought of dire consequences.

Meantime, Nick, our landlord, began putting pressure on us. He wanted more sales, always more sales, and he was almost violent in his demands. So when an unexpected call came one evening, Erutan and I jumped at the chance.

"Hey, we got a hot tip!" The voice was a hoarse whisper on the telephone. "The fuzz are hot to trot. They're set to close in on our crop. You guys want some?"

I handed the phone to my husband. "If this is what I think it is," I said, "let's cash in and split!"

It turned out to be, indeed, just what I thought. Some of our acquaintances — they didn't really qualify as friends — had been growing marijuana in their back yard, apparently getting by with it. But time was running short, and they were offering to share some of their crop with us, knowing we could use it well.

Wasting no time, we helped them harvest the bumper crop. Some of the stocks were so big I thought of using them for the flutes I liked to make. It was a touch-and-go situation; the cops could have popped in at any moment to bust us all. But we managed to load my mother-in-law's car, which we'd hurriedly borrowed for the event, practically from floorboard to top, to say nothing of a tightly packed trunk, and we got away before anyone else came. And there was plenty more for the growers to take away.

Without letting Nick know of our bonanza, we managed to cash a lot of it in. I baked cookies and pies, liberally laced with grass, and with a week's diligent work pushing it in various forms, we made enough to buy a used "bug" — a Volkswagen — which we loaded with the remainder of our leafy jade, and split we did, all the way to La Puente.

We knew better than to try to stay very long at my folks' place, so after turning some more of our crop into a different kind of green, we found an apartment in Baldwin Park, and wonder of wonders — Erutan got a job! It was the first time we'd ever attempted to exist like what you'd call "normal."

"Okay, man," my husband told me, "I'll work six months and you work six months. That way it's fair."

I nodded. I'd wait for him to work the six months first, and then see what might happen. Things were cool for a time, for although Erutan didn't exactly dig his factory job, he was willing to hang on to it to keep bringing in some bread.

But it was too good to last, and within a very short space of time, all of it fell apart. First, the car broke down, and Erutan had a tough time getting to work. Then our square landlord began to ride him for playing his conga drums at odd hours, warning him to knock it off. The guy had the nerve to complain about Erutan's guitar, too, and he likewise didn't seem to appreciate my own efforts on the flute. It was too much for us — too much discipline. With a non-running car, a sorehead landlord, and much too stuffy an existence for us to stick with, it was time to move on.

I had only one question: "Which way?"

Erutan looked at me with that careful, speculative way he had. "How about Laguna Beach?" he said.

I considered, trying to copy his deliberation, then nodded. "That's cool," I agreed.

And so, via the thumb as usual, we were on the road once more. At Laguna, we discovered that most of the hippies were holed up in the hills — a series of caves situated in nearby canyons.

"Only way to go, man!" were words from one of our kind who lingered to rap a bit after he'd bought some of the remaining supply of grass.

Most of the caves, we found upon exploring them, were already occupied. We'd lived to ourselves long enough to know we relished that aspect more than moving in on others. So we kept climbing and looking, and finally at the bottom of one of the deepest canyons, we came upon a large cave — room enough for five or six families. It wasn't the greatest shelter in the world, open as it was, but it was empty, ours for the taking. It was our kind of thing.

We'd hike into town each day, up the hills and down again, and panhandle our way to whatever kind of food we chose to eat. It was winter by now, and nights were cold and wet. We slept on a rock, and when it rained, the wind blew the wet on us till it seemed we were doomed to freeze. Yet, this was home, and despite its discomforts, we dug it more than the squarehead landlord's apartment we'd tried in Baldwin Park.

Then one day Erutan had a stroke of good fortune. "Boy, did I luck out today!" he told me when we met to begin our daily return trip to the cave.

His "luck-outs," I'd found, were not always that great.

"How's that?" I asked cautiously.

"I ran across this crazy dude with a ton of acid," he said enthusiastically. "He gave it to me for a joint — one single joint!"

"How much," I inquired, "is a ton?"

"I didn't even count it up," Erutan said. "I just took it and ran before he changed his mind." Then he carefully opened the sack he was carrying, and I knew enough about acid for one brief peek to convince me.

"Why, there — there must be several hundred bucks' worth!" I exclaimed.

"See what I mean?" he said. "You remember the dude — the one acted sort of weird the other day, with the knife."

I certainly did remember. The guy came from San Francisco, he said, and some of the things he'd said had convinced me I didn't want anything to do with him. I thought, deep down, about all the reports on the Zodiac Killer up there, and I wondered if maybe Zodiac hadn't ventured further south till the heat was off in the bay area.

"Where'd he get it?"

"Found someone's stash," my husband said. "Wanted to move it in a hurry." Then, with a grin, "For just one little joint. Crazy!"

So we lived high for a while. At $3.00 a tab, we had enough acid to bring in lots of bread, since there was a plentiful market for it.

And of course we kept on panhandling; it was simply our way of life.

I'd wear my loin cloth to town, but I didn't dare go topless as I had in Seattle. I also wore bronze Indian bells on my ankles. It was one more way to attract attention, something I'd been searching for all my life.

During the six months or so we spent in Laguna Beach, I kept on reading whatever books I could find on Eastern religions, and I went frequently to the Krishna temple at the base of the canyon where our cave was located. But my quest brought me no nearer the truth...peace...happiness...security I sought than I'd been before. And I'd spend the rest of the day mooching whatever I could on the street corner, along with continuing to peddle acid or whatever other dope we could get our hands on, including what was left of our Seattle grass crop.

There came a day when I wasn't feeling so good — stomach upset — and Erutan said he'd go into town and panhandle for us while I stayed at the cave. I slept awhile, and awakened to a strange noise of bottles breaking. I'd no more than gotten to my feet than I saw a couple of cops throwing all our water containers and anything else they saw down into the canyon below us.

I shivered. We had a big bucket of dope in the cave, and I knew what would happen when they found that. But I had no choice but to confront them.

"What're you doing here?" one cop asked when he saw me.

With my bells and pouches and weird costume, he probably thought he'd run across a witch. "I live here," I said proudly. "I might ask you the same question."

They weren't there to play games. Quickly they searched me, not being too careful how they did it, but coming up with nothing. Then they went on with their systematic wrecking of our meager household. My husband's conga drums, all the boxes of our belongings went the way of the broken bottles — pitched down the canyon.

There was only one good thing about it. While they continued their search and clean-up, I casually sauntered over near the entrance, and then beyond. Quickly, I unfastened and abandoned my ankle bells, and took off running. I was one girl they weren't going to bust that day, not if I could help it. I spent the whole day among the canyon rocks, careful to keep out of sight of the fuzz.

The next morning after gathering up what we could of our scattered trappings, I was nauseous again, and since it had been happening rather regularly, I decided it was time to pin it down. So I hiked to town with Erutan, spent some time in a doctor's office, and confirmed what I'd suspected. I was pregnant. I'd never given much thought to that possibility. In all the time I'd spent with Chuck Sipe, now Erutan, and before that the occasional sexual adventures I'd accepted, I'd never bothered about birth control. As far as I was concerned, nature could take its course. And nature had, at this point, chosen a course I didn't especially welcome. I'd be afraid to take more drugs now, of course, not while I was pregnant. I didn't want to take chances with the effect they might have on my unborn child.

My husband, surprisingly, was more excited than I was, "Are you really going to have a baby?" were his words. And when I nodded a forced-smile confirmation, "Hey, that's neat!"

We were on our usual street corner when I looked up to see a recognizable face. The recognition was mutual. "Thought you got away from us, didn't you?" It was one of the cops who'd stripped our cave the day before. "Guess I'll have to take you in now."

"What for?" I began to cry, and it wasn't any put-on. The shock of verifying my pregnancy had left me on the verge of tears, anyway.

"You know well enough what for!" the cop sneered. "I can throw the book at you for half-a-dozen violations!"

"Please!" I pleaded. "I — I'm pregnant! I can't take getting busted — now!"

"Good story!" the cop snapped. "Got any more like it?"

I kept on crying, then played my trump card. "You can't take me in," I said. "You can't prove anything! You can't prove I was there yesterday, because I'll swear I wasn't!"

My husband picked up the cue. "She was here in town with me all day yesterday," he nodded.

Glaring at us, the cop turned on his heel and stalked off. He could have taken us in for panhandling, probably for half-a-dozen other phony reasons, but maybe he just didn't want to hassle it. Anyway, when we slowly climbed up and down those hills to get to our cave that night, I made up my mind.

"We've got to move out of here," I said, thinking about the time when I'd be far enough along for my pregnancy to make me awkward and heavy. "I can't take this climb much longer."

Erutan looked at me in his speculative way. "Can't get out without making some bread," he said practically. "You bring the bread, then we can think about it."

"I'd like to go back to Joshua Tree," I said dreamily. "That's a neat place!"

"Bread!" my husband commanded.

By then, I knew most of the tricks, and the knowledge that I was pregnant brought them to mind. So the next day, I checked in at the welfare office with my tearful story all worked out.

"I've already got one baby," I moaned, "and Doctor Rogers told me yesterday there's — another one on the way." I sobbed a little. "I've run out of money and..."

"Where's your other baby?" the clerk broke in.

"With — with a girl friend of mine," I lied. "I don't know what I'll do!"

"Wait here," the clerk said, and returned shortly with some forms to fill out. I sweated through them, hoping my story was convincing enough to pull it off.

There was another wait, and then the clerk came back with a beautiful piece of paper in her hand. "This will cover one month's welfare payment," she said. "You'll have to keep in touch with this office on a regular basis, otherwise you won't get your check."

"Oh, thank you, thank you!" I turned on the tears again. "Thank you very much!"

I looked at the check: $148.00! *Joshua Tree, here we come!* And back at the cave that night, I confronted my husband with the cash. "Got the bread!" I said. "Let's go!"

He reached for it, counted it carefully, then looked at me, apparently not in the least interested in how I'd managed to cadge that amount of money. "That's cool!" he said. "Gather up the stuff."

A series of uneventful rides took us to our desert destination, and once there, we found the Town House vacant and for rent, so we used part of the welfare cash to make it our own. Thompson's Ranch, we were told, was no longer in existence. It had been sold for taxes, or something. And the once-thriving hippie colony had

thinned to only a few like ourselves. It was pleasantly exciting to
be in a civilized house again.

But the nausea I'd been suffering not only continued, it was now
accompanied by an acute depression as I visualized being
hampered in all my future activities by the tiny body growing
within me. I felt strange, different from any way I'd ever felt
before. I fought with Erutan, almost constantly. It was like it had
been when we were incessantly at each other's throats at Joshua
Tree before...at Placitas...at Seattle...and just about everywhere
we'd ever gone.

Then, one day came a knock at the door. Opening it carefully,
always expecting the worst, I screamed for joy. "Jennie!" My old
friend was back; she was always popping up; and I loved her for it.

She was living in Joshua Tree, it turned out, with a guy named
Tom, and the grapevine had gotten to her with the word that
Erutan and I were holding the Town House.

We had a lot to talk about, but when she was gone again, the old
depression set in. Even the knowledge that she'd be back soon
didn't help keep up my spirits.

A few days later, in the midst of a typical fight with my husband,
I decided perhaps a brief change of scene coupled with something
else to take our minds off each other might be helpful.

"Let's go get my stereo at my mom's," I said. "Jennie said we
could borrow her car anytime we wanted."

He looked at me and slowly nodded. "That's cool," he agreed.
We were on our way within an hour.

When we drove up to the house in La Puente, Erutan said, "Well,
I'll wait in the car." He didn't like my parents, of course, and since
the feeling was mutual, I didn't argue. So I went in, chatted with
Mom for a time, and decided that since she was the only one at
home, my husband might want to join us.

I got back to the car to find two men hustling my husband into
their own car.

"FBI, ma'am," one of them said when I walked up to protest.
"This man your husband?"

"Y-yes."

"We're taking him in for draft-dodging," he said. "He's under
arrest."

"D-draft-dodging?" I hadn't ever given much thought to Erutan and the draft. I'd just assumed the army didn't have any particular use for marijuana-freaks, so I'd never questioned him about it.

"You'll be notified about his status," I was told. And the car roared away with my husband and the two men in it. I can only guess that they'd staked out my mom's place, knowing Erutan was married to me, and therefore was likely to show up there, sooner or later.

There wasn't any use crying about it to Mom, so I took the stereo we'd gone after and headed Jennie's car back to Joshua Tree. Two days later I got a brief note from my husband; he was in Los Angeles jail; could I get some money and bail him out?

I tried; goodness knows I tried; but it was no use. I couldn't raise anywhere near the five hundred dollars it would take to spring him. I barely scraped up enough to enable me to go and tell him I couldn't do anything about it. Being six months pregnant didn't help a bit. I could only assure him that I'd be standing by, waiting, whatever happened.

It didn't take long. He was given a choice: the army or prison. Telling me about it afterward, Erutan said he thought it over carefully. "I decided it'd be easier to get out of the army, one way or another, than it would to break those bars," he said. "So I chose the army, so I could claim conscientious objector. They took me anyway."

Take him they did — to Fort Lewis, Washington, in the area where he'd been when he registered for the draft. Later, when he'd received a notice for induction, I learned, he'd just torn it up and ignored it. So the FBI guys weren't kidding when they nabbed him for draft-dodging.

I kept the house in Joshua Tree, but after a few weeks, I talked Mom into giving me the money to fly to Washington to see my husband. His mother, I learned, had moved to another house, so I reluctantly agreed to stay with her. Then I found out that in order for me to visit him at the army base, I had to have a marriage license. I sent to New Mexico for that. The reply shocked me.

"We have no record in our files of the marriage of Charles Sipe and JoAnn Myers," the county clerk wrote me. "Neither name appears on our records." I thought back — had we given our new names, which we'd begun using there at the Placitas commune? No, I recalled our mentioning at the time that we'd have to use our real names to make it legal. No record! The so-called minister who read our vows was even phonier than I'd thought!

But despite her strange habits when not at school, my mother-in-law was right on. "Only one thing to do," she said. "We'll have to arrange a pass for Charles and get you two legally married." Then with a smile at my bulging middle, "It's about time!"

The first time I saw Erutan there in Washington, I got quite a jolt. With his head shaved and the beard gone, he was a different person. He looked like a sixteen-year-old boy. Lost were the long hair that had given him, for me, a guru image; the scraggly, unkempt beard that I'd come to accept; he'd lost his touch. He was ugly!

But after the initial shock which had me ready to turn and run the other way into nowhere, I got hold of myself. "Don't worry," I told him. "I still love you, even without your long hair." His reply was a word I'd rather not repeat.

The second wedding was quite different from the first. There were only four of us — Erutan, me and his mother and father. They'd been divorced, of course, but still lived in the same area. And my husband's father, as I'd discovered during our earlier stay in Seattle, was just as different as his mother...or as my husband himself.

I explained it to his mother later. "We went to see him just one time," I told her, "and he propositioned Erutan — Chuck — to let him make some pornographic films of us."

"He's really flipped!" She shook her head. "Did — you do it?"

"No way!" I told her. "Erutan wanted to do it, but I dragged my feet. He finally gave up on it."

I told her then why so many times we'd argued and fought over his crude behavior, his often preferring pictures to the reality of physical expression. "You're kidding!" she said. And when I assured her I wasn't, "You pood kid. You really married a winner, didn't you?"

By then it was too late, for our second marriage ceremony, performed in a small Presbyterian chapel in Seattle, had become a matter of official record. Like it or not, I was Mrs. Charles (Erutan) Sipe, soon to be the mother of his child.

So now I could go see him, now that the marriage was legal and on record. Not only that, I could fulfill what I knew would be one of his fondest wishes, now that he was restricted to conformity with army rules and regulations. The big bowl of potato salad I made him would just hit the spot; I knew it. I knew it because I tossed a whole lid of marijuana into it. Needless to say, he dug it — the first high he'd been on for quite a spell.

I went back to a lonely Town House in Joshua Tree, once my brief visit was over, and while I could have gotten stoned on pot the way I would have if my husband was with me, I didn't really have any desire to hide behind the haze of burning grass. I knew Erutan was trying in every possible way to get out of the army, but I wasn't sure he'd make it. And I wasn't sure I could make it through the coming ordeal of having my baby. I wasn't sure at all. I'd decided to follow Erutan's "natural" philosophy and have a totally "natural" childbirth, and as time went by, my deep-inside fright built up into a roadblock of black fear.

My visit to the Seattle area hadn't been that exciting, but the hours dragged by so slowly at Joshua Tree that I grabbed a plane the minute my first allotment check from Erutan and the army arrived, and back I went. I'd have been better off to have stayed where I was.

"Here's what I want you to do," my husband said in that slow, deliberate, and forceful way of his. "You go back and start screaming and acting weird until someone comes to pick you up. Then you can plead insanity."

I didn't understand. "What for? What do you mean?"

"They won't let me out just because you're pregnant," he went on. "But if you act goofy, if they declare you insane, then they'll have to let me out. Don't you get it?"

I got it all right, now. He was getting real panicky about this army business. But as usual, I was to be the one who got the show on the road. I knew better than to argue, though.

"You think it'll work?" That was as far as I dared go.

"Sure, it'll work. It's got to!" The desperate note in his voice almost convinced me I'd try his scheme — almost.

Back at Joshua Tree, however, acting crazy was the furthest thing from my mind. The closer the time came, the worse I felt, and the cloud of murky fear building inside me brought me close enough to insanity without faking it.

In the end, I chickened out on the natural bit I'd planned, and I also got cold feet on my original intention to leave my mother out of the picture. Being alone was too much. I went home two weeks before the baby was due.

Somehow, the two weeks went by. How my family was able to stand me, I am not sure, for I know I was touchy, cranky, just plain mean. So what else was new with me?

Two weeks. Three. Four. The baby was two weeks overdue. Another week and the doctor who was to deliver the baby delivered an ultimatum instead.

"We'll have to go to induced labor," he said. "I want you in the hospital this afternoon."

So I checked into Heartland Hospital in Baldwin Park, not sure whether I cared or not what was about to happen to me. At this point, I was numb with waiting, with worry, with the same bitter loneliness I'd tried to dodge all my life. Would my new son, Na-shon, or my new daughter, Shemyiah, make any difference? I'd had plenty of time to think about names during those five weeks of waiting at home. And strangely, I'd dug into the family Bible to come up with these possibilities. I didn't worry that Shemyiah was the Biblical name for an early prophet; I liked the name and that was all that mattered.

There is no point in recounting the agony of the next twenty-four hours. Those mothers who have experienced heavy labor for an extended time know well how it was; those who have gone through quick, easy births are fortunate not to know; and no man could understand.

At 8:35 A.M. on September 17, 1970, Shemyiah Nyomi Sipe was born. The exhilaration, the emotional satisfaction of giving birth were missing; I felt relieved — nothing more. Looking back, I can realize I was not really emotionally ready to have a child.

Adding to my discomfiture, each time the nurses brought my daughter for breast feeding, she cried...endlessly. I hated it. It was a bummer.

As so many other times in my life, I felt the inadequacy was me; my daughter didn't dig me. And I didn't know what to do. I was skinny almost to the point of emaciation. The birth had involved numerous stitches. I was too sore to walk. But after three days in the hospital, they sent me home to my mother's, with a program I was to follow. Do this; don't do that; none of it made sense to a barely 19-year-old girl who wasn't ready for motherhood.

And whereas at the hospital, the nurses had treated me with respect and had tried to help me through a difficult time, at home it was the exact opposite. If I'd felt rejected at home before, I was super-rejected now. On the other hand, my baby was strictly the queen of the realm. You would have thought this was the first baby ever born.

I wanted to get to know my baby, to make her realize I was her mother, to overcome the constant crying that kept everyone on edge.

A typical scene found me holding, cuddling Shemyiah, hoping to comfort her. Enter my mother.

"What are you doing with that baby? Here — give her to me!" And because I dared not hold that tiny body against the strain of my mother's demands, I would release her, only to have a parting slap flung at me from the doorway. "You stupid thing, you!"

I'd known before that I was just trash. Yet, my daughter — my own flesh and blood — was an exalted being. I simply could not understand. It was all right for me to try to cope with her at night. I'd be up all night long, trying to still that tiny protesting voice. So of course I was ill-equipped to handle her during the day. Breast feeding, I felt, was a bummer. A visit to the doctor's office produced a formula, which Shemyiah promptly proceeded to throw up, time after time.

More than once, I left the house. I left running, the best I could with all the soreness that still plagued me. I felt like running away, never to return, but I always went back — back to my baby, back to the interminable tug-of-war.

About a week after I'd gotten home from the hospital, Erutan, as a new father, was granted a brief furlough. His reaction to his newborn daughter was typical — a careful look, a silent shrug of the shoulders that said, "Big Deal!" and a turning to other things. The things were how could he get away from the stifling atmosphere of my parents' home, how could he get out of the army, and how could he find a fresh supply of pot and get stoned?

But before he could get away from us, Jennie arrived on the scene, her eyes alight with a new experience.

"I've found it!" she exulted the minute we were alone. "Onjya, it's the answer you've been searching for all these years!"

I needed news like that. "What?" I asked eagerly. "What is it?"

"The Family!" she said. And then, at my puzzled look, she filled in the blanks. "You know, they call them the Manson Family. Part of them are on trial at the Los Angeles Hall of Justice. You've read about them?"

I tried to bring fuzzy thoughts into focus. I'd paid scant attention to what was going on in the world, for a long time. But I did recall mention of the Manson Family. I remembered that more than a year before, movie actress Sharon Tate and four other people had been murdered, and then a couple of other persons were done in the very next night. I'd heard that the Family leader, Charles Manson, and several others were on trial for those killings. I recalled, too, that at the time they were arrested, the word "hippie" had been liberally associated with the accused persons, so I'd figured they were innocent. But what was Jennie talking about now?

I nodded, and Erutan likewise acknowledged awareness of the Manson trial. "So?" I said.

"It's beautiful!" Jennie went on. "The Family is like — you wouldn't believe! They've found the real truth, Onjya! It's all love, beauty, and peace! The girls are all so neat. They serve all the men the way it was meant to be. They're..."

"What's that to us?" My husband interrupted Jennie's enthusiasm with his usual deliberate calm.

Jennie threw him a quick glance, then turned back to me. "They're totally different. They even walk and talk different," she explained. "They're — like one big family. Cool. With it. In." She shrugged, running out of words. "I love them all!"

If Jennie loved them all, I would love them all, also. I knew it. But what could be done? "Could I — we — join too?"

Jennie's dark eyes sparkled. "They'd love to have you!" she confirmed. "That's why they're so great. They're full of love, especially for anyone who..." She let her voice trail off, not needing further words to pinpoint our problems.

Wordless, I looked at my husband; he looked back at me. Then, from Jennie, "Why don't you guys just split. Come on out and meet them. See for yourself!"

Split! For me, it was a magic word. The stresses of the past week at home had left me eager for whatever change could be made. I turned to Erutan. Was this the answer we'd been waiting for?

"Why not?" he said. "What's to lose?" Deep down, I could sense what he was thinking. Anything to get out of the army, even desertion. Maybe this really was the answer.

Then, a terrifying thought: "What about the baby?" Could I leave my child behind — leave her to the kind of fate I'd suffered at the hands of my own parents?

"Bring her along!" Jennie smiled. "The Family loves babies! They'll help you bring her up right!"

It was all I needed. "We'll go!" I confirmed. "But we'll have to sneak out. My mom's got her hooks into Shemyiah so deep that ..."

"No problem," Jennie said. "You guys be ready, say 11:30 tonight. Okay?"

I nodded, and my husband gave the word. "We'll slip out," he said. "See you then!"

10

Manson Philosophy —
Power Vibes!

I had visions of having to clamp my hand over my baby's mouth that night when it was time to move out, but for once, she was asleep. She did not stir when I picked her up and wrapped her in a blanket for the trip. I had no idea where we were going, when or if we would return, or what to expect. But I knew it was time to split, and I was supremely glad we were leaving. Whatever new problems might come could not, I felt, be any worse than those we'd leave behind.

At precisely 11:30 P.M., Erutan and I softly climbed out the window of the bedroom, and at the same moment, a car without lights rolled into the driveway. Until that instant, it had all seemed unreal that we could actually escape from the heavy atmosphere of what had once been my home.

"You cats ready?" It was a hoarse whisper drifting to us out of the night. A moment later, we were in the back seat of the car, quietly backing away. No more words had been spoken; there was no need for them. Jennie, I saw, was sharing the front seat with a young man I'd never seen before.

Where we were headed, we did not know, nor care. The aim was to split, and that aim was being accomplished. From now on, I'd have my baby to myself — no more interference, no more "unfit mother" comments. This was cool.

Ever inquisitive, I had the presence of mind to check an occasional street sign. I wanted to have at least a general idea where we were going, where we'd end up. It didn't take very long. I saw enough signs to know that when the car rolled to a stop, we were either in or near Duarte, a Los Angeles suburb which, like La

Puente, lay generally to the northeast of the metropolis.

The hideout, for that's just what it was, had belonged to a young married couple, I learned later, who'd known Thomas Walleman (known to the Family as T.J., the Terrible) for some time. What they didn't know was that he was connected to the Manson Family. So when T.J. asked if a couple of friends could crash, there was no objection. But as always happened with the Family, they simply moved in and took over. The two who came to crash turned into indefinite larger numbers, and before the owners realized what was happening, not only the entire house but their lives as well were totally changed. When we moved in twenty-five people were drifting in and out.

So when we arrived, there was no great to-do about it. With what Jennie had told me, I was openly curious about what we'd find. Love, beauty, and peace, she'd said. What more could anyone ask?

"Hi. I'm Bo." The slender, brunette girl was looking at me with the same frank appraisal I was giving her.

I nodded and Jennie put her hand on my shoulder. "This is my good friend, Onjya," she said, "and her husband, Erutan. Oh, yes — this is their baby, Shemyiah. She's just two weeks old." Jennie gestured toward a long-haired young man, who seemed disinterested in what was going on. "This is T.J.," she added with a smile. "T.J., the Terrible."

I didn't see anything terrible about him. In fact, I didn't see anything unusual at all. But I could feel it! The minute we stepped inside that house, I felt a super-strong, all-possessing power vibe — hard to describe, except that the whole atmosphere seemed charged with electricity...or something. I glanced at my husband, wondering if he, too, felt the same vibes. I couldn't tell. He was "casing" the place, and I knew his nose was sniffing out the possibility of pot. If it was there, he'd be into it, and soon.

Then, as though on signal, others began to arrive, and one by one, Jennie introduced them to us. Mary Brunner — slim, red-haired. Gypsy — real name, Catherine Share — dark-haired and pretty, with piercing brown eyes. Clem — real name, Steve Grogan — thin-faced, with a straggly beard and unkempt hair that reminded me of my pre-army husband. And later, other people I vaguely remembered having heard of somewhere, no doubt because their names were often in the papers and on TV — Ouisch — real name, Ruth Ann Moorehouse; Squeaky Fromme; Sandy Good; Kitty Lutesinger; Sue — real name, Susan Bartell.

It was Gypsy who started a rap session with me, as Jennie sat by, an interested spectator. "There is no wrong in this world," Gypsy began, and her convincing manner had the ring of truth in it.

"Everything is good. You just have to accept it the proper way." Her dark eyes bored into mine. "Whatever you do is what you are supposed to do; you are just following your own karma."

I nodded, holding my baby close and rocking her back and forth to keep her quiet while I absorbed this new philosophy. "No one owns you," Gypsy continued. "You own yourself. God is there in you, and you are the way. This is Charlie's word."

It sounded fascinating; it sounded like the truth I'd been searching for all my life. I waited eagerly for more of these words of wisdom.

"Take your baby, there." Gypsy's warm smile told me of her all-encompassing love. "She doesn't belong to you. She is her own self, her own person. You belong to yourself, she belongs to herself. You shouldn't try to possess her."

"I see what you mean," I said. "That was always the trouble with my mom. She wanted to possess me, and it didn't work. Then, with Shemyiah..."

"You could be you, no matter what," Gypsy interrupted. "Even around your mom, and then she wouldn't try to possess you any more. You're your own person, Onjya, your own person."

Truth — at long last. And faced with this truth, I suddenly felt evil, that I had been misguided all my life, that I wanted — I really wanted — to get right!

"You have to become unprogrammed," Gypsy said then. "And you have to let your baby be unprogrammed. Otherwise, she'll grow up with the same hangups you have, and that's wrong! Becoming unprogrammed to the things of the world — that's Charlie's way."

Charlie's way. How marvelous! I had only to look at my own messed-up life to realize how much better it would be for Shemyiah, who could grow up the right way, unprogrammed. I wanted to meet Charlie Manson, to hear for myself his profound pronouncements.

"What about Charlie?" My question slipped out before I had time to really think about it. "He's — in jail, isn't he?"

Gypsy nodded, then with a confident smile, said, "But not for long. He'll be out soon, and we'll all retreat to the desert."

When I arrived, I was wearing a long white Indian skirt with lots of embroidery-work on it, along with a similar multi-colored blouse. I couldn't help contrasting my own rather gaudy clothing with the simple well-patched levis worn by Family members. I also liked their ponytail hair style, worn by both sexes. It seemed right, just as the words Gypsy had laid on me seemed right. It was all truth, and I dug it.

Then, although he'd barely acknowledged my presence when he arrived, the Family member named Clem suddenly stalked into the room, knelt before me, and without speaking a word, reached to unbutton my blouse. His action not only took me by surprise, it was done in such a matter-of-fact way — almost like a ritual — that I had no word of protest. I just sat there fascinated, wondering what would come next, making no objection when Clem removed the blouse entirely, leaving my upper body exposed; as usual, I'd worn no bra.

Laying the blouse aside, Clem carefully surveyed my torso, then turned to Gypsy. "Hey!" he said with enthusiasm. "Charlie would really like her!"

Gypsy nodded in agreement. "Yeah!" she said.

I wondered. With trying to nurse Shemyiah, my breasts were milk-swollen, considerable larger than normal. Would Charlie like me later, too?

It all seemed so right. They were so open with each other. There seemed nothing wrong, even when Clem exposed my body. Yet, neither did it turn me on especially. It was all so very heavy that I didn't have time to wonder about it. It was strong, overpowering, like being under the influence of an inescapable power. We were all like little children, it seemed, and there was no wrong.

From Gypsy, then, another smiling admonition: "Just remember — do the opposite of everything you've been taught," she said. "That's the only way."

I nodded, grateful for having found the truth at last. Then, from another part of the house, someone called my name.

"Onjya!" And when I looked around to see who wanted me, the follow-up words, "In here!"

Gypsy pointed toward the hallway that led to the home's two bedrooms, and also the bathroom. "There," she said.

I stood up, handing Shemyiah to Jennie and not bothering to retrieve my blouse. If this was the way of life for the Family, it would be my way of life, too.

I headed for the hallway, wondering what would come next. At the bathroom door, Clem took my arm. "Come on in," he said, not bothering to shut the door after himself.

And then, continuing the child-like naturalness of Family life, Clem led me to the stool, where he proceeded to relieve himself, at the same time doing some quite personal exploring of me.

"Hey," he said then, "have you ever been touched like that before — by a guy?"

The Family was open, honest. There was only one way to answer. "Sure," I admitted.

It was a mistake. Quickly, Clem withdrew his hand, uttered a disgusted obscenity, and strutted out of the tiny room. I wondered where my husband was, how he'd have reacted if he'd known. I needn't have wondered. When I went back to the living room to put on my blouse and retrieve my baby, I saw from the corner of my eye that Erutan had found his coveted stick, and was not only enjoying his deep whiffs of grass, he was also caught up in conversation with Mary Brunner. I could just as well have been a thousand miles away. Although I was not completely aware of it at the time, Erutan had listened well to Gypsy's explanation of the Charles Manson philosophy. With each his own person, not belonging to anyone else, his responsibilities to me and to his daughter were washed out. He was no longer responsible to us. He had already, to put it bluntly, disowned us.

Back in the living room, while I was trying to quiet a now unhappy Shemyiah, Jennie posed a question, as much to Gypsy as acting head of the Family as to me. "Why don't you just stay?"

I shrugged. I was as yet unaware of my husband's attitude. It would depend to a great extent on his wishes, for unlike him, I did not consider our ties as severed.

But at that point, he wandered into the room. "Want to stay here with the Family, Erutan?" Jennie asked.

Slowly, deliberately, my husband looked around the room, and I knew he was tempted. He was due back at the army base in Washington within a few days. Which would he choose?

From the corner where he sat propped against the wall, T.J. tossed in some heavy thoughts. "You don't want to go back to that crazy army place," he said. "I can get you a fake I-D — no sweat. Better stick around."

Everyone, it seemed, focused then on Gypsy, who would make the final decision. She looked at my husband, then at me and the baby. Then, her face radiating the smile I'd noticed when I first saw her, she voiced her approval. "Why not?" she said. We were in!

By now, it was early morning, but there was an important move to be made. "I'll have to get the baby's stuff — from home," I said. "I didn't know what to expect."

Gypsy had a ready answer. "You got out," she said. "Can you get back in?"

I thought it over. "I — think so," I said. I'd never tried to sneak into my folks' house in the dead of night.

"We're used to that," Gypsy said then. And within a few minutes, with T.J., we were enroute back to La Puente, where we creepy-crawled back into the house, picked up the things we needed for the baby along with some personal stuff of our own, and were back in the car on the way to Duarte with no one at home the wiser.

My own embroidered Indian skirt, I found next day, was nowhere as elaborate as some of the embroidery the Family members were into. There were elaborate vests for Charlie and the other guys. But far surpassing everything else was the velvet gold cape they were fashioning for Charles Manson for the day when he would be released from jail, and would rendezvous with the other Family members in Death Valley's desert.

Lined with a parachute to insulate against hot or cold, this beautiful cape was topped with a braided hair collar, made from locks clipped from Family members. It was different, unusual, and it seemed to radiate power vibes of its own — just that rare combination of cloth, human hair, and handiwork.

Death Valley and the coming Revolution were constant themes for discussion by the Family. Charlie Manson, it was said, would

lead the chosen people to their underground refuge deep in Death
Valley, where we would await the call from the black man who
would triumph over the whites, but would then seek the supreme
aid of Manson, world leader. It sounded far out, but it sounded
like truth, especially when I heard tapes of Charlie's own songs.
They seemed deep with hidden meaning, and while I didn't
understand, I felt I didn't need to.

The unquestioned unity of the Family spoke for itself. It had to
be truth! And if I'd had any questions during those first few days
of sharing with this unique group, they were answered with the
arrival of Brenda McCann. Brenda, I found, was as I hoped to be,
in response to this new-found way of life: totally unprogrammed.
She seemed to be living in a dream — yet it was a dream that was
truly reality. It was reality that was different, beautiful, filled with
love. Whenever Brenda would come around me, there was a
radiance that could not be denied. Charisma, they call it today.
Charisma was hers.

For one thing, Brenda — alone, among all the others — seemed
to accept me totally, with no reservations. She made no judgment
of me. Looking back to my limited knowledge of the religions of
the world, I could see Brenda McCann as almost a saintly being.
She was totally free, totally happy, and in conformity to the
Manson philosophy. She had been deprogrammed until her mind
was completely open — no fears, no hangups, no problems. She
didn't even walk...she danced. She was what I wanted to
be...super-free!

And if I'd had any doubts about the Family before, Brenda
chased them all into an obscure corner. She was the convincer.
"Now I really want to join!" I said to myself. Everything I'd picked
up on before, I felt, was either an out-and-out fake or else simply
hadn't come through on the glowing promises I'd seen in their
concepts.

The Family believed "There is no law." I had been trying to
convince myself of that for years with my rebellious ways. The
Family members told me Charlie had set them free. The hangups
they had inside were gone. He was able to break through that. Yes,
this was for me. The Family made sense; the world didn't make
sense to me.

But much as I wanted to accept the Manson philosophy, much as

I wanted to become unprogrammed, there were still problems to be solved, hurdles to be crossed. Everyone of us was equipped with buck knives, for example, with a blade that snapped out by a switch of the hand. Many members also carried hunting knives. And sometimes there'd be weird goings-on. They'd pretend they were killing each other...with the knives. There was an evil cast to it, yet with Brenda beside me, evil wasn't evil any longer. It was like it was all purely right.

The Family was deep into leather crafting, which was something I'd shared with Erutan for many months. Soon I had my own moccasins, as well as my own knife, and I'd join the group as we'd sit together, carefully honing our knives to a razor's edge. Sometimes, we'd dance with the knives, demonstrating as part of the dance our skill in drawing the knives from their leather cases at our belts.

Erutan, I found, was now of less than no use to me. He had accepted the unprogrammed idea without question, as well as the "no one belongs to someone else" theme. So while I still had the tenuous security of being Mrs. Charles (Erutan) Sipe, it was actually meaningless.

As the days went by, I came to more and more confusion. Brenda, of course, I could lean on. But I wished for the actual presence of Charles Manson, so I could experience for myself the marvels of his mastery. I wanted to be open, like Brenda, yet I couldn't seem to get with it. I felt I was evil. I felt I was programmed, that I could never be myself. Because I was evil, and because I wanted the truth in me above all else, I would have even let them kill me. It was a time of total bewilderment.

I saw the truth, I thought, in those around me, and I wanted it for myself so badly I knew not which way to turn. It was a constant battle in my mind — is this right, or is this wrong? Despite the assurances of those around me — Jennie, Brenda, the others — I remained uncertain, unconvinced. Inside of me kept echoing, "It's wrong!"

I could sense — and see — evil around me. Yet, those around me said that evil was good. This posed the final question: was I going to give myself over to evil? Was I to accept Satan?...for that was what it meant to me. Was evil God? Was Satan God? Who really was God?

Deep inside me, something was saying, "No — it's not good! All this is not for you, Onjya!"

I wanted to shout, "Get out of here!" I wanted to throw off the shackles that held me back from complete acceptance of the "Evil is good!" philosophy of the Family. I kept trying to shake it all off by doping up with drugs that had long been a part of my life. But it was no use. The same persistent doubts nagged at the corners of my mind.

I didn't know it then, of course, but the forces of good and evil were having a tug of war deep inside me. God was trying to set me straight, and I was telling Him to go away! He, and He alone, was keeping me back from giving my heart and soul to Satan. It was a trying time for Onjya Sipe...a time when I literally and physically sweat a swirl of flowing perspiration.

What was I to do?

11

Revolution —
Escape to the Desert

I couldn't sleep. I couldn't eat. I began to wonder if I could ever think straight again. I was totally exhausted — physically and mentally — and I didn't know which way to turn.

So I turned to the person who'd shared much of my distorted life. No, not my husband. Jennie. Good old dependable Jennie who had a way of showing up when I needed her. I needed her now, and she was there.

"I really want to dig their philosophy," I told her, "but I'm not sure. Do you think it's the truth, Jennie?"

She nodded and smiled. "I'm convinced, Onjya," she said. "The things I don't understand, I just figure I'm programmed. If I don't understand it now, I will later."

Beautiful Jennie! If she was convinced, then I'd accept the philosophy, too. But it wasn't easy. I couldn't help noticing that Erutan was trying to make out with the other girls now that he'd found out he was "free." And that continued to bother me, even though it was obvious that his attentions were unsuccessful. The girls would tease, but in accord with Family practice, that was as far as it could go — for now. The idea, I found, was to use sex as a come-on, to make the male recruits stay on in hopes of gaining the favors that were always just one step away.

I couldn't decide what to do. Once, I got Erutan outside alone. It wasn't easy to maneuver that. I laid it on him quick. "Let's leave!" I said. "Let's just go!"

He looked at me in that slow, deliberate way. "No," he answered. "I found these people, and I'm not leaving!" Then, turning away as though he was shutting me out of his life forever, "I don't own you any more and you don't own me!"

"But what about all the knives and creepy-crawling and..." I didn't really want to say it, "the murders! What about all the — evil?"

Erutan shrugged his narrow shoulders. "There is no evil," he announced quietly, echoing the Manson philosophy. "There is only love."

I wasn't through, even though he was obviously trying to get away from me. "I know they talk love and all that," I said, "but is it really love when..."

"I'm staying!" he interrupted, walking away. "You do what you please!"

The finality of his pronouncement made it easier in some ways. At least I didn't have to worry about my husband; I knew where he stood. I could make up my own mind.

The real problem was that I wanted to believe what was being said around me, but that really made me more panicky, for I knew I was lost and I really needed the truth and I wasn't sure how I could get it. I wanted, above all, to save my baby. I wanted Shemyiah to be saved from the world of mistakes I'd grown up in, and I wanted to accept the Family's way as the right one. I knew I'd have to change my whole thinking around.

Back inside the house, I listened while Gypsy, and Brenda, and the others talked of what was to come. "It's getting closer all the time," Gypsy said in soft, confident tones. "Helter Skelter is going to start any moment now. Everything's going to come down."

"What is it?" I asked. "What is this — Helter Skelter?"

She smiled indulgently, explaining it as though I were a child. "It's the revolution," she said. "The black people are going to take over, and we have to get to the big hole in Death Valley, to be ready for Charlie — for the second coming."

That brought up a point I'd wondered about. "Is Charlie really Jesus Christ?" I asked. "Is Jesus coming back. Is that what you're saying?"

Without answering, Gypsy rocked back and forth, a confident smile on her lips. As I'd noticed when we first came to the Family hideout, the air seemed supercharged; there were heavy vibes. Gypsy didn't need to answer. I could sense the truth, and I could only hope that while there might be no hope for me, letting

Shemyiah grow up with the Family would save her from the programs of the world.

At that moment, I was with and for the Family all the way. "Even if I have to kill and do what they do, I'm going to do it!" I thought. "I'll do it all!"

From the other room came a familiar sound. My daughter was pushing her lusty lungs to the limit. I got up to get her.

"Wait!" It was Brenda, my favorite among all the Family members. "Let me show you what to do."

So Brenda preceded me to the bedroom, and once there, she put her face down to Shemyiah's and screamed back at my baby in tones that duplicated the infant's anger.

Smiling, Brenda then turned to me. "You just have to reflect what she's doing and she'll stop," Brenda said, ignoring the fact that Shemyiah was still screaming. "Don't ever talk to her. Just show her what she's doing. She has to remain unprogrammed, so only the men should talk to her — never you."

It made sense, and yet it didn't make sense. I knew I could never scream back at Shemyiah the way Brenda did. I'd be far too embarrassed. But if only the men were allowed to speak to the baby, and her own father refused to speak to her, what would happen? I was thoroughly confused. So what else was new?

"The best thing you can do," said Gypsy when we went back to the kitchen area, "is to get away for a while. You need to go out to the desert and die to your ego." She was speaking to me, but then she turned to Jennie. "You, too, Jennie. It's the only way."

"But what about..." I was about to say, "my baby," but under the circumstances, I wasn't even sure whose baby she was.

"We'll take care of Shemyiah," Brenda put in with a smile. "You guys go ahead."

I looked at Jennie, and she shrugged. An hour later, we were en route to familiar territory — Joshua Tree. If we were to 'die to our ego' it might as well be at a place we both liked.

"What do they mean?" I asked Jennie when we were alone. "Just what is it we're supposed to do?"

"Well," she said, "I'm not sure myself. The way I understand it, we have to get rid of our ego. We have to die to it." She paused, thinking. "We've been programmed, Onjya, and all that has to be removed."

"Programmed." I repeated the word. "What does that mean?"

Again she paused in thought before answering. "It means society has set patterns that we blindly follow," she said. "We've been programmed by our parents, by schools, churches, every phase of society." Another pause. "You have to get rid of all the things that cause hangups," she said. "Like you have to give up things like mother and father, push away all the inhibitions, just blank yourself out."

"Oh." I wasn't sure it made sense, but at least I had to give Jennie credit for trying. I was glad she was with me. She was an island of hope in a sea of uncertainty.

We spent three days at Joshua Tree, but when we went back, I don't think either one of us had changed in the slightest. If we were to die to our ego, it would have to come later on. Maybe some day we'd find out what it really meant.

Back in Duarte, life went on, and at times, it was a strange life, to be sure. The evenings were the interesting times, for everyone would gather around, and we'd talk about the experiences of the day. This was the time, too, when the Family members would come from their vigil at the corner near the Hall of Justice in downtown Los Angeles. They'd shower and clean up, and we'd all share together what was going on...Sandy, Squeaky, Ouisch...they were beautiful, always shining, always smiling. I loved them all.

The Charles Manson miracles were recounted, and I could only gasp as I learned what kind of genius they thought he was. According to Gypsy, for example, Charlie almost got out of jail at one point after he'd been indicted for the Tate-LaBianca killings. He got out of his cell, past the guard, and was almost free, when he doubted — just once. And once he thought, once he doubted, that blew it. He was simply so aware that he didn't have to think. He could just transport himself wherever he wished.

The Family members spoke also of Charlie healing a man with club feet, just by commanding him to lose them. Then there was the bus in the desert — Charlie would elevate it over rocky stream beds and other places it couldn't possibly maneuver. And when they'd speak of these things, there would be heavier than usual magnetic vibes filling the atmosphere of that house.

I got more information on the coming Revolution, too. There was an immense hole — a bottomless pit — in the desert in Death

Valley, and it was here that the chosen ones would congregate. Charlie was going to pay men to get the water out of an underground river at the pit. He believed there was an underground world there, with people — other escapees who were chosen by God — already living in mid-earth. It was, I was told, a world of chocolate fountains, like a land flowing with milk and honey — a paradise, where the chosen few could get away from it all. There was talk of a tunnel and guns too.

Surprisingly enough, much of this Manson philosophy was grounded in the Bible, I was told, but I never bothered to check it out at the time. I just took their word for it, and though their word was far out, I accepted it as truth — the truth I'd searched for all my life.

It wasn't without reluctance, however. I'd go out on the grass at the house in Duarte at night and talk with Jennie — if I couldn't get Erutan outside, I'd grab her — and I'd rap with her. I was really fighting inside, trying to come up with the answer as to the right or the wrong in what I saw around me.

"Well, the Bible says there'll only be certain chosen ones who will be called," Jennie told me, "and these are the chosen ones."

With mention of the Bible, I'd think, "Now, this has got to be the truth!" But as I said, I never took the time to read the Bible for myself.

Everyone was always giving me different keys to get to where they were. Gypsy, for example, handed me a paper of Charlie's writings, and I dug in on them. But I didn't understand what I read. "Don't think things are so important," was one of his statements. "Get off your kick of thinking you're important, something else is important — nothing matters! No sense makes sense!" It certainly didn't make sense to me.

As for the others, they were determined to make a success of the coming Revolution and the trek to the desert. They were even going to go to a dentist to get some tools, so that when someone had a toothache, they could just pull the tooth out.

It wasn't just a kick. It was vitally important to them. They had hundreds of other details worked out, and the seriousness of it all was totally convincing. It *had* to be truth!

They were certain, too, that Charlie would be freed from jail to lead them to the bottomless pit in the Death Valley desert. The only shadow of a doubt that crept in was the statement that occasionally came up that if the authorities didn't set Charlie free, the Family would go ahead and start the Revolution, and then he'd get out for sure. Never was there the slightest hint of hopelessness in their plans.

Charles Manson, I learned, believed that the popular Beatles musical group in England were actually the four angels referred to in the eighth chapter of Revelation. And to follow that up, he himself was the fifth angel, who, in the first verse of chapter nine, "...sounded, and I saw a star fall from heaven unto the earth: and to him was given the key of the bottomless pit."

The ring of truth, unmistakably! He carried it further: the locusts referred to in verse three were Manson's dune buggies. And the seal of God in verse four "in their foreheads" was the bloody "X" he carved on himself during the early stages of his trial, duplicated shortly after by Gypsy, Sandy, Squeaky, and other Family members. Truth!

Then there was the quotation direct from the Bible, that same chapter nine of Revelation, the twenty-first and last verse: "Neither repented they of their murders, nor of their sorceries, nor of their fornication, nor of their thefts." This, too, was in Charlie's writings, and it was repeated by Gypsy and others. I did not understand; I only knew I must have stumbled onto the ultimate truth at last, and I threw myself into Family life with all my heart.

And what a life it was. A regular exploit was the daily garbage run. We'd go to a supermarket and jump into the big trash bins and dig out all the fruits and vegetables we could find. That's how we'd eat; Charles Manson had taught the Family members, "Why not eat it? Why waste it?" There was always something to scrounge in our fairy tale world. It was no wonder we were all very trim and thin.

Besides that, there were food commodities available from the welfare office. Brenda and Clem would take Shemyiah with them and claim her as their child and get flour and cheese and other provisions, often then loading up a car with the stuff so they could take it to Death Valley to stash away for the coming Revolution.

"Isn't that neat? They just give us all this food!" Brenda's eyes were shining in her always-happy fashion when she made that remark after a welfare office trip. Unprogrammed...just the way she wanted to be...free, like Adam and Eve before the first sin. Was the Family, too, without sin? I couldn't be sure. I wanted to think so, but I wasn't sure.

Erutan, I knew, was not without sin. Openly, as if I didn't exist, he'd scheme to be near the other girls, even Jennie. What, if anything, came of it, I do not know, but he was always trying. Turning me off even more was his attitude toward our child. When he did bother to look at her, it was a glance at a stranger. And if I dared bring it up, I'd get a fast brushoff. "I don't belong to you. You don't belong to me. Get lost!" He didn't even bother to include the baby in his declaration.

Like the others, he was often a puzzlement. In one of our nightly Family rap sessions, Erutan suddenly came up with a direct question. "Gypsy, if you guys didn't commit those murders, who did?"

I blinked. Out of the blue, for no apparent reason, here was my mixed-up husband, acting straight. Why?

But it didn't bother Gypsy. "The black people did it," she replied casually. "The Black Panthers." And then, to lend even more authenticity, "I've been talking with them on the phone, and they tell me it's going to start soon."

"What?" Chuck asked. "What's going to start soon?"

"The Revolution! What else?" Then she calmly turned to me. "With your blonde hair, Onjya, you'll be the first to go."

I thought, "Wow!" I looked at Gypsy's black hair. *The first to go.* Did that mean the first to go to the desert? Or the first to go — another direction? I was afraid to ask. But from that time on, because of what Gypsy said about the black people being responsible, I was sure every black I saw knew all about the Revolution, and I consciously tried to avoid any contact with them.

Although I'd sworn to have no more contact with my folks when we sneaked away in the middle of the night, after a week of October had gone by, I realized there was an important piece of paper at home that I needed the worst way — my monthly allotment check. So I called Mom on the telephone.

"Where are you now?" That familiar, rising pitch voice. "What kind of a mess have you..."

"Everything's cool, Mom!" I reassured her. "We're living with a real nice — Family."

"I'll bet!" Almost a snarl, then a completely altered tone. "How's — how's the baby?"

"She's fine," I said. "Mom — about my allotment check. Could you send it to..."

"Where are you?" she interrupted before I could get the address out.

"I'm trying to tell you," I snapped. "Send my check to..."

This time the interruption came from the nearby kitchen table where T.J., the Terrible, was sitting. "Tell her you've got your own life to live!" he said. "She's still trying to program you."

I finally managed to get the address repeated for Mom. "Where's that?" she said.

"Just send the check, Mom!" I ordered, and hung up. Surprisingly, a couple of days later, there it was — a beautiful $100 check, and a beautiful reason for the Family to maintain their open arms for us. I managed to buy a good supply of leather goods to work on before I pooled the remaining resources into the Family treasury.

It was a rainy October, and there were days when we'd all be stuck inside the house for hours at a time. I never knew what to expect; some times were good, others unbearable. And always totally unpredictable!

I was using my knife to trim some leather one day, and for no reason at all, Clem grabbed it out of my hand. In doing so, he nicked himself, and the sight of blood freaked him out.

"Wow! I'm never touching *your* knife again!" You'd have thought the knife was alive, that it had used its edge with knowing intent.

But that was typical of Clem, where I was concerned. Ever since that first night, he'd really had something against me. Everyone else seemed to like me — except Clem. I wanted him to like me too, so it was just a natural thing to try to shine him on. It was so obvious that Clem wanted attention, and the other girls gave him the notice he needed. But he always turned cold to me.

Once when T.J. was sitting next to me while we were sharpening our knives, Clem came over and began rapping. It was evident what he was doing — using T.J. to talk to me, indirectly. And what he said sent shivers up my back.

"You know how it is out in space," he said, and there was an almost unbelievable undercurrent of hate in his tone. "When there's static, the Martians destroy it! They don't fool around. Wham! It's gone!" Every word dripped dislike...for me. I wondered. Did I wrongly read another word...murder...into what he was saying?

The message wasn't lost on T.J., however. "Knock it off, Clem!" he said. I concentrated on my knife. I wasn't sure I wouldn't need it for protection. And I was grateful to T.J. for shutting off Clem's attack.

The Manson philosophy of the women being slaves to the men was a way of life in that house. It was our role to do everything possible for them — from lighting their cigarettes to feeding them to answering other physical needs. Not only that, we were expected to be so aware that we'd read the men's minds, and answer their needs before being asked. The women were soulless, mere sex symbols. No wonder Erutan dug it!

I could only guess that until I finally accomplished the necessary feat of dying to my ego, I would be unable to function as a slave as adequately as the others. And I wasn't sure I cared if I made it or not. One day, I'd be with them all the way; the next, I'd long to put it all far behind me...the confusion, the doubts, the fears. Yet, I stayed. What else was there to do?

Among the better hours were those spent listening to Charlie Manson's tapes. There was one song he'd written, and when he'd sing in that plaintive voice, with the girls chiming in live with chorus parts, I knew they had to be the ones chosen of God, like Jennie had said.

"From the Valley of Death they come," went the song, and the girls would come in with a chorus of "Ah-um...ah-um!"

"Far much brighter than the sun.
Ah-um...ah-um!
Can't you see the great stone?
Far much better than the slave stone...
No wrong...no wrong come along."

I wasn't sure what it all meant, but I dug it. I liked the way they sang. Gypsy, I'd been told, was also a talented violinist, but she had put all that behind her.

"Gypsy, why don't you practice your violin like Susie does?" The words were a mockery as Gypsy recalled her mother's attempts to get her to stay with her training exercises.

It was a standard conversation, all of them recalling their resentment of parental control. "It's really neat, being away from all that rot!" was a typical remark. "Free from being programmed. Free to know the truth!"

The truth! One day, I'd be sure I'd found it. The next day, I'd doubt. And life with the Family went on.

Shemyiah, of course, was not the only youngster in our group, although she was the youngest. There was ten-year-old Katie, who most of them called Heatherstone; six-year-old Joey — they called him Sunstone; and four-year-old Nicky, better known as Soupspoon, and probably just a bit retarded. They were the children of one-time Family member, Dennis Rice. So the place was seldom quiet. There was always a flap of some kind with the kids, aside from Shemyiah's noisy protests.

Like the day Soupspoon got into our knives, and the first we knew, he was a bloody, screaming mess. Most of the others just looked at him, all except Bo, who seemed to be a part of the Family, yet seemed different. I finally concluded that, like me, she hadn't yet died to her ego. I'd have stepped in to help then, but I wasn't sure if I should. It was one of those days when I wasn't sure of anything.

Bo quietly picked Soupspoon up, took him to the bathroom and washed out the cuts, and comforted him while she bandaged the wounds. I believe if Bo hadn't taken over, the others would have let the poor kid bleed to death. He would go through frequent tantrums, and their standard treatment was to grab him by the legs and swing him in a circle until he'd stop screaming.

Once when Squeaky came in from the vigil at the Hall of Justice, Gypsy included one of the youngster's tantrums in her report, and received a typical reply. "Just keep it up," Squeaky advised, "and pretty soon all his fear will just flow out." Her red hair and eyebrows above her hazel-tinged eyes seem to be all blended together by her freckles.

It was the same theory as my screaming back at Shemyiah. There was one of our evening sharing times — talking about what had happened to everyone during the day — when Brenda's report shocked me. She'd stayed at the house while the rest of us were out foraging.

"Yeah, Shemyiah and I had it out today," she said, acting like she'd won a big victory. "We screamed and fought it out all day till the end." I didn't say anything, but I couldn't help wondering; if her technique really worked, would it have taken all day? The uncertainty of it all bugged me.

An even more definite uncertainty that came up from time to time was the way the vibes surged around me. The change from love to hate could be instantaneous, with no words even spoken. I felt deep inside, without ever voicing the cold sweat that haunted me, that Clem or almost any other Family member could wipe me out without thinking twice about it. It was strange, but I felt it was they, not I, who were the weird ones.

How else could you classify T.J.'s action the day he came into the bedroom where several of us were rapping. I'd just changed Shemyiah's diaper and cleaned her up. Without a word, T.J. took the dirty diaper, scooped his fingers into it, and began eating, a grin on his face.

Even Gypsy was turned off. "Oh, T.J.!" she began, but he held up a quieting hand.

"You want to experience everything, you know," he told her. "It's just another experience." And he grinned wickedly. Weird!

Despite her frequent screams, Shemyiah seemed to thrive, and she was often the center of attention. "Just look at her!" they'd say as she lay naked before them. "Isn't she strong!" She was, I felt, a truly beautiful baby, and I couldn't help a surge of pride; she was solid, superb.

My deep-seated fear of that unpredictable undercurrent of changeability kept me from protesting an action that shook me up good, almost to the point of panic. One evening at sharing time, Clem took Shemyiah and balanced her on one hand, waving her through the air in all sorts of gyrations, yet not letting her fall. It was almost like a miracle, and it became a frequent ritual. Never once did he drop her, though my heart was often in my mouth. It became another convincer that life with the Family was truth; I was sure some higher power must be holding my baby there in Clem's enchanted hand.

It was not long after Halloween, a night when a bunch of us

dropped acid and T.J. ended up getting busted for a siege of fiendish laughing in the post office, that Gypsy laid some frightening news on us.

"We're going to have to go for awhile," she said. "Spread out." Whether or not it had anything to do with T.J.'s bust — he'd gotten out of jail the next day — it seemed the cops were getting hot on the Family's trail, for one reason or another. "You're still going through your ego changes." She turned to Jennie and me, glancing across the room to include Erutan, as well. "And you might foul it up for us, because when you're going through ego death, you don't function right."

I nodded. What else could I do besides accept this announcement, strange though it was? I knew I hadn't died to self.

"So what we want you to do," Gypsy went on, "is go up in the central state area so you'll be close to Death Valley and find a place where you can keep the kids till the Revolution breaks." She smiled confidently. "It won't be long!" she said.

I glanced at my husband. He didn't want to be with me, I knew, but I also knew he was strictly a follower as far as Family life was concerned. If Gypsy said jump, he'd jump.

"You guys go out and 'X' yourselves," Gypsy said then. "Put an 'X' on your forehead like ours, and go wait for us. Then we'll meet you out there."

"We'll have to find a place first," I put in.

Gypsy nodded. "So what are you waiting for?" she said pointedly. "Tomorrow may be too late!"

As so many times in our abrupt moves from one place to another, Jennie and Erutan and I were on our way to Lone Pine, a town nestled between the eastern slope of California's Sierra Nevada and Death Valley. Only this time, we were equipped with one of the Family's cars, and we had Family funds to keep us going.

"Are you going to 'X' yourself — like they said?" I asked the question of Jennie, while Erutan drove.

"I don't know. Are you?"

I shuddered. The ugly scars many Family members wore didn't appeal to me, yet if they marked the chosen ones...

"Not me!" I was surprised at my husband's words. "Not natural!"

There it was again. Everything had to be natural. For once I was glad. I'd stay natural, too, I decided — if I could.

I wasn't sure what we were looking for when we got to Lone Pine, but the general idea seemed to be that we'd be hiding out from the cops, so we'd have to be a little cagey about the whole thing. Erutan, however, was used to that sort of activity, and within an hour after he'd left us to nose around with some discreet questions, he was back.

"Got just the thing," he announced triumphantly. "There's a good cave, about three or four miles from here."

"Cave!" I thought back to the wet and cold and cops throwing things out at Laguna. It wasn't a pleasant thought. And the children! How could we care for the children in a cave?

It took a while to find the place. We walked on a winding road through the desert hills, following a dry stream bed for a time, then threading our way around giant rocks. The car, of course, was left behind at the side of the road back to Lone Pine. The final mile was strictly a walking expedition.

Erutan suddenly stopped, surveying the terrain around us. We'd reached the edge of a canyon, with a rock-strewn face stretching in a fairly sharp slope above us. "Ought to be about here," he said thoughtfully. Then, pointing, "Yeah. That's it."

Blending into the rock was a wooden door, and to its left, I could see a dirt-splotched window. "They claim this was a hideout for AWOL's during the war," Erutan said then. "Let's take a look."

He pulled the door open carefully, laying it back against the rock wall. Slowly, we stepped inside. I thought I knew what to expect, but I was wrong. This cave was in no way like the one we'd occupied in Laguna. It was tight, secure. And its walls were beautifully swirled in natural formations that were almost breathtaking in their orange-tinted splendor.

"Wow!" I put my hand on Jennie's shoulder. "I never saw anything like this before. This is neat!"

Jennie's face wore a sickly smile. "I don't know." She shook her head. "Living in a place like this..."

"This is it!" Erutan declared. "Let's get back to Duarte and get Shemyiah and the other kids."

I was shocked. He'd actually spoken our daughter's name — the first time!

12

The Step —
Death to My Ego

By the time we got back to the house in Duarte, it was evident that the Family was anxious to split the scene. So our news of a good place to take the children was happily received.

"It's a really neat cave," I told Gypsy eagerly. "We can stay there as long as we need to. It'll be fine!"

She glanced nervously around her, seeming to have only half-heard my report. "That's great," she said, without enthusiasm. Then, "What's that?"

A car door had slammed at the front of the house, and Gypsy was near panic. Part of the reason, I figured, was that she was pregnant, and I knew some of the reactions this could cause. "That" turned out to be some arriving Family members, but Gypsy's paranoid reaction to every noise made me feel it was high time for sure to get the children to the cave before something drastic and unexpected happened.

Since we would not need a car where we were going, Mary Brunner and Bo were designated to drive us back to Lone Pine with the children, so I was glad a van was available to transport the nine of us on the trip — our two escorts, Erutan, Jennie, and I, plus the four kids. It was a restless trip, with Mary concentrating on the way on a list of items we'd need at the cave to set up our living quarters.

Among the things loaded into the van before we left was an Indian-type wooden back carrier for Shemyiah — something I was later grateful for many times. It would enable me to tramp the trail to Lone Pine and back to the cave with hands loose to help make the way over the rougher spots.

Before we left, there were repeated instructions from Gypsy. "Remember, you have to 'X' yourselves, so you'll be ready," she said, without explaining what it was we were to be ready for. I assumed she meant the coming Revolution. "We'll meet you out there and all go over to Death Valley together — later."

Mary's list, it turned out, included leather and foodstuffs, but little in the way of sleeping or other accommodations in the cave. We'd just have to make do with the blankets and other supplies we'd loaded at Duarte, but things hadn't been all that comfortable at the house, so the prospect wasn't too discouraging. Besides, packing everything in on our backs led to a lighter-the-better outlook.

From the time we arrived to settle in, I could tell that Jennie wasn't too happy with the cave. And she wasn't the only one. The other kids were excited about it, but Heatherstone (Katie) almost immediately showed signs of discontent. Being the oldest, and being used to quite a few others around her, I could see how she felt, so I tried to give her special attention.

"I still don't feel up to cutting an 'X' in my forehead," I told Jennie in confidence after we'd straightened things around as best we could. "Maybe if we just cut off all our hair, they won't notice."

She shot that idea down. "They'll notice, all right," she said, "but cutting the hair is a good idea. That'll show we're with them, even if we don't do the 'X' bit."

So I chopped off all I could of Jennie's hair, and it was pretty weird. I meant to leave one of those long tails of hair, but it didn't work out too well. But Jennie got even with me, because what she left me wouldn't have won any beauty contests, either.

The November weather was cold outside. Inside the cave, the temperature was probably in the low or mid-sixties — not warm enough to be entirely comfortable, but at just the same level all the time. It didn't get any colder at night, nor did it get any warmer in the daytime. Our water came from a nearby stream, but it looked clean and tasted good, as mountain water usually does. We discovered that another couple lived in an old shack a mile or so away from us, but they didn't seem interested in any socializing, so it didn't mean much.

I wanted to keep the youngsters busy and interested, but there were still problems with Shemyiah. She was seldom quiet, and I

was sure it was all my fault, and there really wasn't much to do to
pass away the time. So I suppose it was natural that our nerves
were on edge much of the time.

I was still torn by mixed feelings, especially about Erutan. I
realized now how jealous I'd been, watching him scheme on the
other girls there in Duarte. After all, this was a complete turn-
about. When he was in the army, I'd write to him every day, and
when he returned after Shemyiah's birth, I was sentimental because we'd had a daughter — together. The total change to life
with the Family was almost more than I could take, especially with
his attitude of "Get lost!" I simply wasn't ready to let him go.

On the other hand, I wasn't ready to hold on to him, either, not
the way things were going. One night not very long after we'd
settled into the cave existence, I began thinking about how he'd
acted around the other female Family members, and the more I
thought, the madder I got. I felt super-hurt; he was my husband,
but he didn't want to be my husband, and if that was the way it
was, there was no reason for him to keep on living.

I grabbed my buck knife. A sleeping Erutan could go on
sleeping forever. I'd see to it.

But he wasn't asleep. Before I could plunge the blade into him,
Erutan grabbed my wrist so hard the knife clattered to the stone
floor of the cave. "Hey — what's got into you?" he yelled. "You
gone crazy?"

I struggled, but his grip was a vise. "Let me go!" I protested.
"I'm gonna kill you!"

"You're crazy!" he declared. "You've gone clear off your
rocker!" Still clutching my wrist, he carefully kicked the knife to
the far side of the cave.

Realizing I'd blown it, I relaxed and began to cry. I couldn't do
anything right; it had always been that way with me, and here it
was that way again.

"Go take a walk!" my husband ordered. "Get your head
swabbed out!"

Nodding as he relaxed his grip, I found a jacket and headed for
the wooden door at the cave entrance. The children were asleep, I
noticed, and I was glad they hadn't witnessed our little confrontation. It was bad enough for my husband to know I'd flipped.
It would have been worse if the kids had learned it, too.

The chilly night air didn't really clear anything up, but it did make me think about my problems as I stumbled out over the desert rocks. And the more I thought, the more confused I became. My husband: I had him, he was there in the cave with me, but I really didn't have him because he didn't really want me any more. My baby: I had her with me, but I really didn't have her because I just couldn't get it together with her because I couldn't get it together with myself. My sanity: had I ever really had something that could be so defined? I doubted it.

The problem, although I'm not sure I recognized it at the time, was that after being with the Family, my mind was so demolished that I couldn't even remotely relate to anybody except them and the weird way of life they pushed. I was on my way to being exactly like them, and anybody else who got in my way was clear off the beam and had better split because I couldn't even talk to them. Taking the knife to Erutan was just an expression of Family philosophy, as far as I was concerned.

I had quite a conversation with myself out there under the desert stars. "It's the truth, Onjya. You have to accept it!" My one self wanted to swallow what I'd seen.

But my other self wasn't sure. "What do you mean, truth? Do you want to give yourself over to the devil? Is that what you want?"

"Well, if Charles Manson is Jesus Christ, how could he be the devil, too?"

"That's all part of God's plan!" my opposite self said. "So if it's God's plan, it has to be the truth!"

I hesitated. I knew if I gave myself completely over to the Family philosophy, there would be no recourse, no recovery. I would have to accept them on blind faith, and there would be no way to come back to any other reality. Something deep inside was holding me back.

"It's the devil! He's working on you. First thing you know, he'll swallow you up." I shuddered, and not entirely from the nippy night air. Where was the truth? What was it? Had the hand of the devil been on mine when I held the knife ready to spill my husband's blood?

For some reason, I thought back to a time some weeks before when our Family group had shared a lot of acid, mixed into a quart of organic apricot juice. Several of us had journeyed to Laguna Beach, knowing we could easily stock up on LSD and other drugs, but after we dropped the acid, everyone was so high we were almost all wiped out.

Someway, we made it back to Duarte, and once there, I really grooved on Family feelings. Suddenly, it all fell into place for me. Around me, the others were still high on the acid we'd consumed. But I felt I had come down; I felt, as I'd never felt before, that I needed Charles Manson by my side. I looked forward eagerly to the time when the truth would set him free from the shackles unjustly binding him within prison walls, when I'd find from him the truth I needed so much. I began to cry because he wasn't beside me as I wished.

High as she was, Gypsy looked at me and shook her head sadly. "Too bad," she said. "Her mom is really sitting heavy on her head."

Emotion, the showing of feelings, was taboo with the Family. It would never do for me to be so weak as to break down in this fashion — a fact which I realized, making me want to melt into the floor and disappear. If I'd had access to a gun at that moment, I'd have turned it on my empty head, just to get it all over with.

And now, in the desert night, these and other thoughts chased across my muddled mind. I was ready to cry again, as I had that night in Duarte, as I had tonight in the cave when my try at murdering my husband was thwarted. But crying was weakness; crying was my mother sitting heavy on my head; crying was not for Family members. I was a Family member; therefore, I dared not cry, even alone in the desert.

Suddenly, I felt the familiar presence of a lifetime partner — the insecurity I'd known as far back as I could remember. I wanted my buck knife in my hand; security was a knife I could use if my husband didn't straighten up and fly right; security was knowing the Family trusted me to watch their children; security was a cave in the desert, and my steps now turned back to that cave. Security was the Manson Family and I was part of that Family and I'd best not forget it!

Having come to this conclusion, I no longer felt I needed to use the knife on Erutan. I crept silently back into our abode to take my place beside him on the cave floor. What was there to be afraid of? I had found the truth. The truth was the Family. All was well.

But it didn't last, of course. Not many days later, there were visitors, and I learned that word had gotten back to the Family. Obviously Erutan had told someone — perhaps Jennie — and someone had told someone else, and the presence of Gypsy, Mary, and T.J. was the result. There was unaccustomed nervousness in their sidelong glances at me that told me word of my knife-wielding escapade had leaked.

"Whew! That's quite a trip!" Gypsy, heavily pregnant, was winded from the walk across the rocks. Then, glancing around the cave, "Quite a place you guys picked."

"It's cool!" I said, smiling at the double meaning.

"Better than outside!" Mary put in. Our weather had turned bitter; it was really frigid in the open.

It was T.J.'s turn. Glancing at the two girls who'd come with him, he turned to me, almost embarrassed. "Hey, Onjya," he said, "like we found another place that's even better — for the kids." He fidgeted for a moment, apparently trying to find the words he wanted. "We'd like to take them with us, and then we'll meet you guys in Death Valley — like in a couple of weeks or so."

Gypsy, her dark eyes fixed on me, nodded. "We'll keep in touch, let you know when," she confirmd.

"Why don't you let us take Shemyiah, too?" T.J. put in then. "That way, we can keep the kids together, and we'll all join up as soon as the way's clear."

"It'll give you more time to die to your ego," Mary Brunner said, smiling at me. "You've got to do it, you know!"

I knew the children didn't dig the cave-life, and the thought of being relieved, for a little while, of my problems with Shemyiah was inviting. But I wasn't sure. Was I a terribly unfit mother to entertain such thoughts? I turned to Jennie, who'd been at Lone Pine the night I tried to knife Erutan, and had since been in and out of our cave life on an erratic basis. She didn't like it, and preferred to find some place else to stay. She'd returned an hour or so before the other three arrived that day.

Jennie smiled at me and nodded her approval. But there was one other person who had to be consulted. Erutan. Despite his disclaimers, he was my daughter's father. I looked to him, wondering what he thought of this new proposal.

For once, he was watching Shemyiah, evaluating in that slow, deliberate way of his the matter of our child's future. Watching him, I had mixed thoughts. I wanted to do what was best for Shemyiah, above all else. And being able to use this means to save her from the programs of the world — to avoid for her the miserable results of my own misguided upbringing — was definitely appealing. Then, almost imperceptibly, Erutan nodded to me, and I felt my heart leap. We would be doing what was best for our baby; we would even be doing good for God. I was sure of it.

"She'll be better off," I said. "After all, it'll only be for a little while."

If I had only known!

13

Cave Life — Confusion, Crazy!

To my surprise, for I hadn't thought in such formal terms, Gypsy sat down and began writing out a paper authorizing the Family members to remove Shemyiah from our presence.

"We have to have your permission, of course," Gypsy smiled disarmingly. "Makes it all legal, and everything."

I wondered. If I signed it, would it be like signing my soul over to the devil? My thoughts were interrupted before Gypsy completed her writing.

"I want to go along, too," Jennie said. "Onjya and Erutan will be better off alone. The," she paused, and I had to wonder if she, like my husband, felt I'd flipped, "ego death will be easier for them if no one else is around."

It was a cop-out, but I didn't care. Things had to be better for us, with the youngsters no longer our responsibility. It couldn't hurt having Jennie elsewhere, too. Gypsy, her scribbling completed, handed me the paper.

I started gathering up what few things there were to send along with the children, including the back-rack for carrying the baby. We stood in the biting cold and watched them trudge away. I wasn't sure if it was the wind or regret that urged the tears down my cheeks as the group disappeared beyond the rocky horizon.

Back in the cave, I tried to think what the paper I'd signed for Gypsy had said. I couldn't remember; I'd signed my baby's life over to someone else, and I couldn't even recall the terms and conditions that had been spelled out concerning the transaction. Already, second thoughts were setting in.

But Erutan, from whom I'd have welcomed some personal

attention at that point, didn't seem the least perturbed about what
had happened.   In fact, he was bent on living up to his
responsibilities to the Family.

"Well," he announced, "I'm going to go out to the desert and die
to my ego. I'm not going to come back till I'm dead!"

It was a brave, sensible thing, I felt. He was duplicating the steps
of our leader — Charles Manson — who I recalled had undergone
the crucifixion experience while on an LSD trip in this same, or at
least a nearby, desert. It was there, in Death Valley according to
the Manson legends, that Charlie had undergone the final death
himself. It was therefore right and proper that Erutan do likewise.

My husband let the door to the cave close behind him, and there
I was...alone...cold...hungry. There was no food. The Family had
quietly gathered up everything in sight for their own journey to
wherever it was they were going.

"No!" I thought. "I can't face this! What am I going to do?"

I thought about Erutan's parting remark, which I'd chosen until
then to ignore. "You better do the same thing!" he'd said before
slipping out.

Now, thinking of it, I thought, "Oh, wow! Maybe he's right!"
For the walls of the cavern seemed to be closing in around me.
Perhaps I needed the great outdoors, with no barriers, no enclosing
stone stockade to pin me down and restrict my every move.

From the moment the Family had gone with the children, I'd
had heavy feelings. I was, I was sure, going to hell, for I was
eternally evil. The others, I felt, were on the right track; they were
heaven-bound, but I was so lost that no one could help me. That
was one reason for my giving up Shemyiah so readily. I wanted
her to make the scene in heaven, too, not to follow me the
other way.

Now, these heavy feelings were more burdensome than ever. I
wanted to flee the cave, to bolt into the desert and let the cold air
wash me clean of the sin I was burdened with. Yet, I took the time
first to let my mind wander through a maze of blame for those
who'd brought me to this sorry plight — my parents, society, the
establishment. They were all instruments of the devil, I felt, and
they had all condemned me to this unearthly fate from which
there was no escape.

I recalled a Charles Manson watchword: "Thought is the

invention of the devil." And here was the devil programming my thoughts.

Shemyiah was gone, I suddenly realized, because the Family wanted to be like her, because of their almost fanatical worship of infants and small children. I recalled when the girls would lie and look at their hands the way babies do, in a concerted effort to achieve a childlike consciousness. I visualized Shemyiah as the Family's leader. In her childish simplicity, she would set the pattern for the rest to follow. It was an exhilarating thought, a satisfying one. It gave me a new confidence that I would do what my husband had done. I could go into the desert, in a different direction, and I could and would die to my ego, once and for all. I headed for the cave door.

It was near dusk now outside, and the temperature was even sharper than it had been earlier. But I was determined. I hastened my steps, hoping I was taking a different route than Erutan had chosen. But I hadn't gone far before more second thoughts set in, prompted in part by the bitter bite of the early evening wind.

"He's stupid!" I announced to myself, slowing my steps. "If he can't die there at the cave, how can he do it out here? How can it matter where you are, anyway? I can't die to my ego out here. I'm too cold! And neither can he!"

Slowly, I turned around to reverse my steps, wondering at the same time if it was the devil who was pushing me to this perverse action. Should I freeze in the desert until my ego was finally dead and buried forever? Or was it right that I return to the shelter of the cave, where I might be cold and hungry but at least I'd be out of this razor-edged wind? Ego-death or not, I'd retreat to the cave to await my die-determined husband.

My teeth were chattering in measured tempo by the time I reached the cave door, and upon swinging it open, I was amazed to find a lighted candle dimly casting dancing shadows on the whorled orange walls of the cave. I had left no lighted candle.

In the blurred indistinctness of the stone-bound room, I made out a familiar form, stretched lazily on the floor, his ever-present stick of grass held leisurely between thumb and forefinger. I turned to him in undisguised disgust.

"I thought you were going out to die to yourself!" I accused.

"Well, I already did," came the answer.

And I thought to myself, "Then, I'm not the only one that's crazy. He couldn't do it all that quick!"

Aloud, I said, "Well, what's it like? How's it feel?"

He looked at me in that slow, deliberate way. "Cool," he said. "From now on, it's strictly you for you, me for me." He nodded his head. "Cool."

"What's that supposed to mean?" I asked, getting angry. Who did he think he was, anyway? "Are you trying to put the split on us again?"

He shrugged. "You gotta be you, and I'm me," he said. "That's how it is."

I slept on the far side of the cave, away from my husband, that night in spite of the constant cool of the cave that had kept us close until then. I felt I'd been betrayed, but if that was the way he wanted it...

The only hope I had was the memory of Gypsy's parting words. "This is the best thing to do," she'd reassured me. "We'll see you out in the desert, when the Revolution comes down." And as further encouragement, "It won't be long!"

We survived the night, but come morning, there was no choice. In spite of the snow swirling past our cave door, we had to find food, and the nearest place for that was Lone Pine. I had no shoes — only moccasins — and I was sure my feet would freeze before we tramped our way into the sleepy little mountain town. There were no words between us; he was he and I was I and that was it. But we panhandled together, and we picked up enough spare change on the streets of Lone Pine to buy a supply of brown rice to keep us for three days.

At the cave, whenever I'd try to initiate a conversation — even a mention of the unpleasant weather — I'd get the same answer. "You don't own me, and I don't own you. That's where it's at!" he'd say. Then he'd clam up and ignore me, like I wasn't even there. There were just the two of us, but he'd built a wall of hate between us. He kept it painfully present night and day.

The frequent trips to Lone Pine were a drag, for there were many times when we'd try all day long and pick up no more than half-a-dollar for our efforts. I suppose there was a reason; with my camouflage coveralls and head scarf, along with pouches, beads, and the ever-present buck knife in it sheath, I probably looked pretty weird, and Erutan was certainly no better. It got so our "Any spare change?" query was harder and harder to use, because everyone scattered before we could get close enough to ask for a handout.

People would grab their kids' arms and scoot the other way when they saw us coming. Those in cars passing by would hurry to raise their windows and lock their doors when they saw us. And finally, came the day when the manager of the grocery store laid the word on us.

"I'm sorry," he said, "but you can't come in the store any more, because you're too dirty. Nobody else wants to come in when you're here."

Just like that. What a bummer! But it turned out to be a small blessing in disguise, for it directed our steps to the welfare office, where we got food commodities that kept us from starving. Now, the problem became carrying the cheese, flour, rice, and other things back across the rocks to the cave. Erutan was always more than willing for me to carry most of the load. He took quite seriously the Family philosophy that the women were to serve the men.

The days, the weeks snailed by. I'd expected to hear from the Family, to be reunited in Death Valley with my baby and the others, for it had to be time now for the Revolution to come down. The Family had promised it. What was happening? Why didn't they return?

I'd had no idea how I'd miss my child when I sent her on her way. I'd been concerned only with her future, with the hope that she would grow up unprogrammed with the evils of the world. Now, without her, I was miserable, devastated. I began crying...every night.

Finally, despite his almost constant silence, Erutan broke down. "Shut up your sniveling!" he snapped. "What's eating you?"

I didn't really want to answer, but the words just slipped out. "Shem — Shemyiah!" I stammered. "I don't know where she is. I don't know if she's okay. I don't know..."

"Shut up!" my husband said. "You don't own her, you know. Just give her up. Forget her. It's evil — carrying on like this!"

So it was evil! I couldn't have cared less. "Well, look, she's my baby!" I cried out through my tears. "I want her. I need her! And she needs me!"

"Stow it!" He turned his back on me, and I left the cave, knowing I couldn't stand being cooped up with him any longer. Outside, I let it all out in a series of screams, until my throat became so tight I could barely make a sound. I pulled the knife from its sheath, looked at it carefully, balanced it on my hand and wondered if I could give it one quick plunge into my heart.

Yet, although I wanted desperately to end this wanton existence, something deep inside held me back. There was something that seemed to want to live. So I threw myself on the icy rocks and tried to renew my screaming. There was nothing else to do.

It was the next day when I discovered, on one of the many shelves that nature had carved into the walls of the cave, an old box that someone long preceding us had left. It was nearly full of rat poison. Once more the urge to end it all — to depart from this unearthly, unproductive existence — seized me. The only question was, how to get it down. I decided the best way would be to dissolve and drink it.

But when I'd stirred it into a can of water and was trying to get up my nerve to force the liquid down, Erutan was suddenly beside me, knocking the can from my hands to dribble over the stone floor.

"No way, man!" was all he said. "No way!"

I was mad — angry beyond all comprehension. It wasn't enough that he refused to share a thankless existence with me. He wouldn't even let me end it all so I wouldn't have to be in his worthless way.

"You———" and I reeled off a series of epithets I'd accumulated through twenty-one years of frustration, ending in senseless screams as I battered my head against the cave wall. I had had it! The pain of hitting my head didn't phase me at first, but my strength finally began to ebb. Fleeing from the cave I sprawled headlong on the desert rocks a hundred yards or so from the entrance. And still I screamed, finally wearing myself out till there was nothing left to push the noise from me.

How long I lay there in the cold, I have no idea. But somewhere along the way, my husband wandered over to where I was, looked

down at me sprawled like an earlier-picked vegetable, and shook
his head.

"You fool!" he said quietly.

I did not respond. I couldn't. I was beyond any sound.

"You're crazy!" were his next words.

And I knew, in my heart, he was right.

14

Shemyiah — Where Is My Daughter?

Crazy or not, the cold soon drove me back into the cave, where Erutan and I slept in our usual opposite areas. He'd refused to come near me in all the weeks since the Family members had reclaimed the children, including our own Shemyiah. And the next morning, exchanging almost no words at all, we set out together for Lone Pine to scrounge whatever we could to keep body and soul together.

In my constant run from reality, I'd called my mother on infrequent occasions, always feeding her a line I hoped would be what she'd like to hear.

"We're doing just fine," I'd tell her. "Shemyiah's growing like a weed. Erutan's got a job, and we have our own place now. Everything's cool!"

Well, it wasn't all falsehood. Wherever she was, I hoped Shemyiah was growing; we did have our own place, if you can call a cave your place; and the weather, the cave, and the atmosphere between my husband and me were all — to say the least — cool!

I'd given Mom our forwarding address as "General Delivery, Lone Pine" some time before, and when I made a routine visit to the post office that day, I found a pleasant surprise. It was another of those long green pieces of paper with some significant figures on it placed there by a U.S. government machine of some sort, and it meant we had another $100 to spend, courtesy of the U.S. Army which apparently hadn't passed the word along to its computer that my errant husband had deserted that organization several months before. I wasn't about to argue with them over my continuing allotment check.

"Hey!" I said to Erutan as soon as I'd converted the single piece of green paper into several other pieces of paper of a different shade of green. "Let's run over to San Francisco and pick up some supplies. It's time we got some things to enjoy ourselves a little."

My husband looked carefully into my face before answering. I couldn't blame him. The night before, he'd declared I was crazy — and rightly so. Now, for a complete turnaround, I felt — and probably looked — perfectly normal.

"Might as well," he agreed, apparently satisfied that I'd flipped back to reality. "Change of scene will do us good."

We didn't even bother to go back to the cave; we just took to the road in our usual hitchhiking fashion, and made our way from east to west across California. We ended up in Berkeley, where the hippie-types outnumbered the squares. But we didn't dig them all that much. Having experienced the freedoms of the Family, I found that everything and everyone else turned me off. They just seemed so out of it. I wondered how they could possibly survive.

I felt I knew so much more than those we met on the streets of Berkeley — or anywhere else. I felt I'd found the truth, and while I wanted to turn others on, my compulsive shyness held me back. The reality of relating to others, after being around the Family, was almost too much for me to cope with.

So after going on across the bay to San Francisco and acquiring some prized possessions with the loot the army had sent, we headed back to our cave existence, but with a new outlook. The trip had done us both good. I'd acquired a real flute — not a make-believe one made of bamboo or marijuana stalks. And Erutan had a real guitar. Plus we both got sleeping bags, the kind that would zip together to form a double unit. We were husband and wife once again.

But before we left, I couldn't resist the temptation to check in with Dan and Louise Watkins, the writer for the *Free Press* of the underground and his wife, who'd befriended Jennie and me on that first trip to the bay area. As usual, they were friendly and curious as to what I'd been up to.

"Not the Manson Family!" Louise's face was horror-struck. "Why — why they're —murderers!"

I smiled at her foolishness. "No, they're not," I explained. "They're neat!"

Dan shook his head. "You gotta be out of your gourd!" he said. "Why those people..."

"It wasn't them!" I insisted. "It was the black people that did it."

"Huh-uh!" Dan was emphatic. "I write! I did an article about it. They found pieces of their hair...fingerprints...they did it!" And when I smiled and shook my head in disagreement, his face turned suddenly cold. "No way!" he said. "Huh-uh! We don't believe your lies!"

So it was a bummer. Dan and Louise, much as we'd liked them, made their choice and it was to turn against us. Typically, it didn't bother Erutan, who just shrugged and began gathering up his share of our belongings so we could hit the road again. I wanted to stay and try to get the truth across to our one-time friends, but I could see it was no use. Erutan's shrug had said it all: "The heck with you guys!" And I could only agree. But at least my husband and I shared the same feelings.

Our return trip to the cave was without incident, and plain as it was, home never looked so good. Once there, however, my old longing to see my daughter and to hold her in my arms and comfort her came back to me. I was soon in tears. Erutan, after accepting me as the wife I was during our trip, was content to ignore me, spending hours picking at the guitar we'd bought on the coast. I tried to bury myself in playing my flute, but the same old haunting thoughts kept nagging at the corners of my mind. Where? Where is Shemyiah? Where is my daughter? The tears would moisten the mouthpiece of my flute till I could get no sound from it.

Days...weeks...went by. Shemyiah was now five months old. What did she look like now? Ours was a weird existence. The vegetarian diet was mainly instant mashed potatoes which we could get from the welfare office, boiled rice, and watercress which grew in the nearby stream. At times I could relate to what was going on around me; other times I was desperate enough to commit murders of the type the Manson Family was accused of — if only I could get my baby back. And through it all, Erutan was content to pass the days with the constant aid of grass or LSD or whatever else was available on the lonesome streets of Lone Pine. Whenever I'd mention Shemyiah, he'd shake his head. "Forget her!" And I'd shake my own head in disbelief.

With the first hints of spring, I could stand it no longer. "I'm going to go look for Shemyiah!" I announced early one morning.

His usual shrug was his reply. And not because I thought he cared, but just in case I didn't make it back to the cave, I told him my destination.

"I'm going to Joshua Tree," I said. "I'm going to look for Jennie." Again he shrugged. If he thought he'd miss me in any way, he wasn't about to show it.

I gathered up my back pack and took to the road. By now, hitchhiking was so much a way of life that I thought nothing of it, although I was careful to size up every driver who stopped, and I enjoyed the reassurance of the knife in its sheath at my belt. I was lucky this time; I was in Joshua Tree by nightfall.

Once there, it didn't take long to pin down some rather startling facts. Jennie, it seemed, had split for parts unknown, and not without good reason. The word was out that the Family wanted to kill her. It seemed she'd told the mother of a young girl in the group where the youngster was. The cops had picked the girl up, and Jennie's name was no longer among the chosen.

But as for Shemyiah, I faced a stone wall. No one had word of my baby, and my hopes of using Jennie as a fount of information were, of course, dashed on the folly of her cop-out.

Not that I didn't think of going to the cops myself. I gave it serious thought — plenty of it. But there were too many complications. Despite his uncaring attitude, my husband was still exactly that — my husband. Any word to authorities was bound to turn up the fact that he was an army deserter. I didn't have the heart to turn him in, especially when I had no assurance whatsoever that it would help me find my daughter.

There was also the clawing fear that if word got back to the Family that any guardians of the law were looking for Shemyiah, they might kill her. Everywhere I turned, others turned away. My husband had told me, earlier, that I was crazy. Now, the people I contacted — after slipping me the word on Jennie — seemed to confirm Erutan's judgment. I returned to the cave from Joshua Tree disheartened, depressed, despondent. If I'd expected a renewal of satisfaction from my husband upon my arrival, that too was lacking. My midday arrival signaled only a grunt from him, as he turned back to the marijuana patch he was carefully cultivating not far from the cave entrance. I might as well not have been there;

even my non-news of Shemyiah was apparently of no consequence to him.

There is probably nothing more eerie in a cave-existence such as ours than awaking in the middle of the night to hear voices at the entrance. A house can be secured; a house has lights outside, a doorbell, other ways of warning or of protection. Our cave had none of these. The voices we heard a couple of nights later struck chills the length of my body. Erutan lit a candle, and in its shadowy flicker, I watched our door slowly swing outward. My hand slid to the ever-present knife at my hip.

"Anybody home?" A familiar voice! I jumped to my feet.

"Mary!" I didn't know the young man with her, but Mary Brunner's presence had always been reassuring, and it was no less so now. She had always been, for me, symbolic of the Family. "How are you?"

"Living on love!" she said in typical Family fashion. "How you guys doing?"

"We're making it," Erutan put in before I could answer. "Everything's cool."

"How's — how's Shemyiah?" Now that there was someone I could ask and expect an answer, I could hardly force out the words.

Mary turned her tender smile to me. "She's just fine!" she said, emphasizing the last word. "She's the most beautiful child in the world!"

My heart leaped at the words, and at the same time, I opened my arms to Mary for a sustained bear hug. It was as though we were sisters, reunited after a prolonged absence.

I lit another candle, and in the dancing mirages of the half-lighted cave, we rapped and rapped the witching hours away.

"Just hang in there!" was the theme of Mary's message. They were encouraging words, and now that I knew firsthand that my daughter was all right, I was suddenly free of fear and the cares that had burdened me. It was as though an anchor had been suddenly lifted from my heart.

Sometime in the wee hours, our talk ran out, and we slept. The next morning, Mary and her friend were impatient to be on the road. "Sorry we couldn't bring you any food or anything," were her parting words. "We're really having a hard time ourselves. Things are really rough right now."

It was the first negative note we'd heard. As I watched them trudge toward the road that led to Lone Pine, a disturbing thought hit me in the face again: I was evil; I was wrong; I was not fit to be part of the Family; they were bound for heaven, while I was headed for hell. I choked back the tears, knowing a true member of the Family would never cry. It was several hours before I realized I'd failed to ask Mary a crucial question: *Where* was Shemyiah? I'd been so relieved to hear *how* she was, I hadn't even asked her whereabouts. I had to content myself with the knowledge that wherever she was, she was still the most beautiful child in the world — Mary's words. At six months old, Shemyiah was the most beautiful baby in the world!

For quite a time, the reassurance of Mary's visit sustained me, but the distressing absence of my baby was a constant fester in my mind, one that would not go away no matter how hard I tried to forget it. I wondered too if my investigation in Joshua Tree had prompted Mary's visit to keep me satisfied and quiet. Only when something completely different happened at the cave did I forget for a brief time the aching problem of Shemyiah's whereabouts. Take the time when two young sheriff's department officers popped in for an unexpected visit. They showed up when Erutan and I were both busy with the marijuana patch, and I had visions of both of us spending some time in the pokey.

They were friendly, as might be expected at the start. "Whatcha growin'?" It was an innocent question, of course. They probably knew exactly what answer they'd get.

"Tomatoes," Erutan said proudly.

The second officer smiled, but there was no indication of disbelief. "Looks like you'll have a pretty good crop," he remarked.

"Hope so." Erutan was never one to waste words.

"You guys live around here somewhere?"

I nodded, pointing to the wooden door of the cave, barely in sight of the level spot where we'd planted our weed. "Right over there."

"Mind if we — have a look?"

What could we say? "Come on."

In the cave, after they'd glanced around and apparently satisfied themselves, the young lawmen strangely paralleled the officers who'd questioned us at Flagstaff when we were running from impending disaster with the hippie clan. "How come you live off out here?"

Erutan shrugged, apparently waiting for me to answer. "We like it," I said. "Back to nature." I knew my husband would dig that answer.

"Kind of lonely, isn't it?"

I nodded. "Sometimes," I said, wondering if I dared talk to them about the Manson Family philosophy. Did I dare reveal that we were just marking time until the Revolution and the departure to Death Valley? Erutan picked it up for me then.

"All depends on what you're looking for in life," he said, an unusually long statement from him. "Onjya and I — we happen to like the wide open spaces, nobody jiving us, nobody to try to push their phony ways on us." He paused, reflecting, and nobody said anything. "It's cool." He nodded, reaffirming our stand.

There were other questions, and when the officers left, they were apparently content that they'd gotten what they'd come for — an insight into the lives of a pair of far-out characters... cave-dwellers, desert rats, whatever. And they never did let on that they knew full well what kind of "tomatoes" we were growing.

When another of those welcome allotment checks came in, I decided it was time to pin down my daughter's whereabouts, once and for all. It was several weeks since Mary had visited us, and I decided to go directly to the one place where I felt I could get an answer. Mary had told us the Family girls were maintaining a vigil at the Hall of Justice in downtown Los Angeles, where the murder trial of Charles Manson and other Family members was nearing an end. It was springtime, 1971.

"Want to go along?" I asked my husband.

He looked at me, thought it over, then shrugged. "Why not?" And we were on our way.

On the streets of downtown Los Angeles, I thought back to Erutan's comments to the cops at the cave, "Nobody jiving us." How right he was! The nearer we came to the bus-like van the Family had parked near the Hall of Justice, the more hate I saw in the eyes of the people we met on the sidewalk. It was frightening! I wished we were back in the seclusion of our cave; maybe it wasn't the greatest spot in the world, but at least it wasn't a world filled with hatred, like here.

At the van, I was shocked at the appearance of the girls, all with shaved heads, all with a prominent 'X' on their foreheads. I was suddenly super-conscious of my own lack of an 'X' and the fact that stringy though it was, my own hair had grown back after Jennie hacked it off some months earlier. Though I was never sure how much I could depend on him, I was glad Erutan was with me.

It was a bald-headed Brenda who welcomed us. "Hi!" she smiled. "Did you know Gypsy had a baby boy? It was the neatest experience!"

Her words reminded me of my mission. "Where's Shemyiah?" I asked.

Brenda glanced to her left, and I let my eyes casually drift there, to see Squeaky staring at me steadily, no smile gracing the freckles splashed over her intent face. Squeaky, I knew, was now temporary leader of the Family in Charlie Manson's absence, and I could sense that any reply would have to come with her approval.

Some signal I did not detect apparently passed between Squeaky Fromme and Brenda, for the answer was quick in coming. "Oh, Jennie took her somewhere out in the desert," Brenda said. "I'm not sure just where."

I knew she was lying, covering up, but what could I do? I wanted to tell them I knew they were out to get Jennie, but I didn't dare.

Then, from Squeaky herself, "Got any spare change, Onjya?"

I could have laughed out loud. Here were the panhandlers, panhandling their own kind. As I turned my pockets inside out as proof, I was glad my husband had our stash tucked securely away.

I thought about the way the Family had moved in on the couple in Duarte, and with this obviously foolish request for funds from us — who had been and were their own kind — it seemed to me that Squeaky's character showed through more clearly than ever before. She was out to get whatever she could, from whomever she could, however she could. I shuddered, sensing that Squeaky

Fromme was capable of the horrendous acts that other Family members were accused of.

With her request for money from me being turned down, Squeaky turned to Erutan, her high-pitched voice shrill in the morning air. "What about you? Any spare..."

"Hey — trial time!" It was one of the other girls. I wasn't sure who'd said it because with those closely shaven heads, their identities were uncertain.

As one, they rose from their pavement vigil and with not even a nod in our direction, filed up the steps to the Los Angeles Hall of Justice. It was as though we had ceased to exist, and I was just as glad.

"Come on!" I nudged Erutan in the ribs. "Let's get out of here!"

Looking back now, I shudder again. It came as no surprise at all to me when on September 5, 1975, Lynette Alice "Squeaky" Fromme became the first woman ever to attempt to kill a President of the United States. She demonstrated, in that brief meeting near the Hall of Justice steps, a capacity that could well include murder. President Gerald Ford was spared by an empty gun chamber and the grace of God, for I'm convinced Squeaky could carry murder in her heart...even for the President of the United States.

We'd had difficulty in finding brown rice in Lone Pine, and since it was the nourishing kind we preferred, we decided to make the Hollywood scene where we knew we'd find it in abundance at health food stores. And Hollywood, we found, had changed since the days when I'd walked the streets there with Janice and Jennie. Hollywood was overrun with Jesus freaks. First it was a young black.

"Brother and sister, we need unity!" he said, and I nodded. That was cool. But then he went on. "And unity comes only one way — through Jesus!"

That turned us off, of course. We weren't ready for anything like that. So we walked on, but I had a thought to voice. "It would be neat though, if it was real. Heaven!" And at that very moment, a vision of what heaven must really be like flashed through my head. It blew my mind! But before I could even mention it to Erutan, others were witnessing around us, and I could sense that my husband was getting uptight about it all.

"Hold it a minute!" he said to one young fellow who'd started talking to us about Jesus. "Don't you know God's in each of us?" And he went on, talking about the freedom to love that was the Manson philosophy, while the young man listened patiently. I could only stand and listen, amazed at how well Erutan seemed to be getting his points across. He was usually so quiet.

But just as I was beginning to feel a glow of elation at the way my husband was converting this young man to our way of thinking — after he'd had his try at converting us to his — some of the other kids in the area got hip to what was going on, and they took him away.

"That was quite a sermon," I said admiringly, as we started across the street.

Erutan grunted. "Burns me up the way these guys think they know it all," he said. "Nobody's got *all* the answers!" I wondered.

We came then to a small group centered around a guy playing the guitar, always a fascinating scene for Erutan, who stopped to listen, only to be immediately surrounded by the witnessing others. It was weird: it seemed like the guitarist was reading my mind or something...that he knew Erutan was a heavy influence on me... that I was weak...that if he could just get me alone...it was as though he knew what was in my heart.

He was singing a really neat song about love, but different from any I'd ever heard. It was about the love of the Lord, and somehow I was caught up in it like in a trance, just standing and listening and listening, unaware of anyone or anything around me. At first he was just looking at me and singing, and it kind of reminded me of Clem in the Family, where there was always a lot of love and everyone was really open and all — just really neat. And then he said to me, "You wanta receive the Lord, sister?"

I thought for a minute, not sure just what was going on, and then he said, "Just get down on your knees!" That, to me, didn't make sense, but I was still willing to listen, to try to determine what this was all about.

Then the next words came. "You know, I used to be just like you!" And I started to get really turned off. He added, "But I had to cut my hair because I'm going to get a job." Well, that did it. Whatever he'd been trying to tell me was gone, as far as I was concerned. If someone had said the right thing at that point, I just might have gotten the message, because our encounter with the Family at the Hall of Justice had set my mind working in a dozen opposite directions. If someone had simply said, "You know, Jesus is the Truth!" I might have turned to Him. But again, I might not.

In any event, I could see that Erutan had had more than enough preaching for one day, so I tugged at his arm. We walked away from the street corner witnesses. As we did, one of the guys held up his Bible and yelled, "We love you anyway, brother!"

"Sure you do!" was my husband's terse reply. And under his breath to me, "What a lot of baloney!"

We picked up our brown rice, had one more run in with a pair of Jesus freaks — neither of whom, unfortunately, seemed to be really with it as far as their true faith was concerned — and we split for Lone Pine. We even turned down an offer of food, because we knew the witnessing would go with it, and we simply weren't ready for more of that. It did set me to thinking, though. If Jesus Christ was powerful enough to turn all those guys on, there had to be something to it. And where did Charles Manson, who claimed to be Jesus Christ, fit in? Was it all phony? Or just Manson? Or the whole Jesus freak movement? I was deep in a state of confusion...and I'd been there before.

By the time we reached Lone Pine and our cave, the marijuana crop was ripe with a big harvest to take. Still bewildered by all we'd seen and done in the Los Angeles area, I could only run from my dilemma by stoking up on pot and playing my flute. It became a twenty-four-hour-a-day obsession, an escape from the reality I didn't want to face. The knowledge that I might never see my baby again — I was convinced of that after the confrontation with Squeaky and the Family — was more than I could face.

There were also other aspects of our life I couldn't really enjoy. Like the frequent creepy-crawl camper-kiping expeditions, when we'd rip off supplies from unsuspecting outdoor types who ventured into our area. Now that pleasant weather was here, we were able to supplement our stocks with all kinds of goodies we'd done without before. It was a true Manson Family foray, but I couldn't really dig it. I shook awhile each time we got safely back within the cave.

About this time, I became preoccupied with the idea that I should find some people — anyone would do — to help get guns and to go scare the Family into giving Shemyiah back to me. It was a weird notion, of course. It didn't get beyond the thinking stage, but it does reveal the state of desperation I'd reached. I wanted my baby back!

I went to a store in Lone Pine — a different one from the shop where we'd been banned — and called home. "Paul," I told my brother, "please come up here and see us. I need help." I didn't go into detail as to the help I had in mind. I didn't need to. If I needed help, Paul would come. He was that kind of guy.

So come he did, within a couple of days, and with a friend, Ross, in tow. I leveled with him, mostly. I told him about the Family, except that I explained the black people had done the murders, of course.

"They're not the way everyone thinks they are!" I said.

"Then what about Shemyiah?" I'd already explained that the Family members had taken her along with the other children. He sensed that perhaps more was involved than I was telling him.

I didn't try to explain. I just let loose with the true purpose of my asking him to come. "Paul, will you help me get some guns together, and some people, so we can go look for her?"

He looked at me and shook his head slowly. Barely eighteen, he had a remarkable perception of life and what it was all about.

"I'm not going to do something like that, JoJo," he said quietly. "But I'll tell you what I will do." He looked at me deeply, straight into my eyes and heart. "I'll tell you a way you can get Shemyiah back. You can turn to Jesus!"

There it was again — the same pitch we'd gotten on the streets of Hollywood — and this time from my own brother! "What good will that do?" I asked, trying to keep the scorn out of my voice.

"Jesus can really make you happy," Paul said with a smile. "He can do anything if you just turn to Him and ask Him!" He added, "He's what you're searching for, you know."

For a fraction of a second, I gave this idea some scant consideration. But only that. I couldn't shake the convictions that had possessed me ever since I'd joined the Manson Family. Whatever Jesus Christ might be able to do, I was sure He wasn't about to do it for me. Unless Charlie himself were really Jesus Christ...

"Not what I need," I told my brother. "Charlie's the answer."

"But Jesus loves you!" Paul went on. "Turn to Him. The Lord can change your life! Become a Christian, JoJo!"

"Me?" I said. "Me — be a Christian? How could I?"

"Sure you can! He can do a miracle," Paul assured me. "All you have to do…"

But I wasn't listening. My mind blocked out his words. "No way!" I was thinking. "Maybe if I'd been brought up different… Maybe… No — no way!" And to emphasize my unspoken thought, I rolled a marijuana cigarette and lit it.

Aloud, I remarked casually, "What about this?" I held up my pot stick. "How come God made marijuana if he didn't intend for us to use it?" Then I rubbed it in a little. "Want to try one?"

Paul shook his head. "That's just one of the instruments of the devil," he said. "That's the devil working on you."

I laughed and savored the smoke. "Then I'm happy with the devil!"

Paul shook his head sadly. "We've got to go," he said, glancing at his friend, Ross. "You wanted me to get some guns and people and help find Shemyiah," he went on. "Well, I won't do that, but I'll tell you what I will do."

I waited, eager to know what alternative my brother might suggest.

"I'm going to pray with some other people that the Lord will bring Shemyiah back to prove He's real," Paul said then. "And I'm going to pray that you'll get saved!"

We were walking out the cave door at that point, and strangely, I didn't get turned off by my brother's promise. I just shrugged. If that was doing his thing, and that's what he wanted…so what?

On the hike out to the road, I walked with them, and Ross began talking to me about the Rapture and all it would mean to Christians everywhere. Again, I wasn't turned off. Perhaps the pot I'd smoked had mellowed me. "That's cool," I told them. Whatever it was, it made me feel good. Not that I had any confidence that what they proposed would help find Shemyiah. It was just that they were so convinced and so sincere that I couldn't help feeling good about having had them come to the cave.

"Remember, we'll pray for you!" Paul's parting words weren't especially encouraging, but I nodded in agreement. Whatever turned him on…

Back in the cave, hoping to maintain my exhilarated feeling, I decided to lean on an old friend, so I dropped some LSD my husband had picked up on our last Hollywood trip.

"Careful," he warned me. "That stuff's got just a wee touch of strychnine in it — good for the nerves, but it might get to you."

But I'd already taken it, and whether it was the knowledge of what Erutan had said, or the actual effect of the poison, I was off on quite a trip, almost immediately.

There were heavy stomach cramps, and I barely made it outside the door of the cave before I began to barf up my insides. Before long, there was nothing left to vomit, yet my stomach continued to retch in a constant pattern of piercing pain that racked me from head to heels. Back inside I wanted to eat some food, so there'd be something to bring up, but I couldn't stop heaving long enough to get anything down. I got so weak I couldn't stand, and still I gagged. There was just no way to get off that trip!

Somehow, I managed to crawl out of the cave into the open, to lie on the desert floor and moan and writhe with the agony of my troubles. I began to hallucinate, a usual LSD reaction, but one that had been missing on this trip. And I suddenly decided that the only way out of this predicament was to make myself get rid of it — mind over matter would make it. Then came the vision.

There were two of them — persons in white — angels? I wasn't sure, but I was sure about one thing: They were real! They were right there in front of me, right there in my real world. And I thought, "They can take this away. I think I'll let them take it away!" All I could think of was deliverance. I was sure they could, if they would, deliver me from the shocking ache that burdened me.

Even as I watched them, they seemed to be motioning upward with their hands. I looked up; blue sky, scattered cotton balls of clouds, nothing else. But as I looked, the pain suddenly passed. Just like that. I brought my eyes back down to an empty desert. My two benefactors also had vanished.

I moved back into the cave. "You won't believe this," I told Erutan in a by-now familiar introduction, "but two angels took me off that LSD trip!"

He looked at me strangely. "Wha-a-at?" he said slowly.

"They did!" I insisted. "Angels! They..."

I stopped. It was no use trying to convey to him what happened out there. Especially when I wasn't sure myself. In some vague way, I tried to connect what my brother had told me with the deliverance I'd gained when those guardian spirits came to my rescue. I couldn't tie them together. I shrugged. What had been had been. I'd let it go at that.

I went back to playing the flute, trying to lose my constant brooding over my daughter's absence in the concentration of making music. I drew on our pot supply, for after that LSD trip, I wanted no more of that. The days and nights wormed along interminably. I thought again of self-destruction; wished there'd been more than a touch of strychnine in that LSD I'd dropped. I wished...

Voices! Again those unnerving sounds approaching our cave in the middle of darkest night. I shuddered, and before either Erutan or I could get up, the door was flung open.

"JoJo — Chuck! You there?"

I jumped to my feet, recognizing the familiar tones of my brother, Paul. With shaking hands, I lighted a candle.

"Paul, what is it? Why are you..."

"You're not going to believe this!" I didn't need the fluttering flame's dim radiance to recognize the smile on Paul's face. It stood out strongly in his eager voice. "Just sit down, Joey! Sit down!"

"What?" I was hoping against hope. Could it possibly be? "What is it?"

I sat.

"Guess what?"

I could have shaken him. I didn't dare guess. "What?" I said meekly, afraid to hope, yet clinging to the thread of promise I thought I'd read into his tone.

Then came the magic word. "Shemyiah!" Paul said, and I jumped to my feet. "They found Shemyiah!"

15

Strung Out — Stripper, Strumpet

I could scarcely contain myself. "Wha-a-at?" I screamed.

Paul's triumphant smile showed clearly, even in the dim candle-light of the cave. "See," he said, "Jesus is showing you that He's real! I told you I'd pray, and look what happened!"

At that point, I wasn't interested in how it came about. All I wanted was confirmation that my daughter was all right.

"Is she — is she..." I couldn't make myself say the words, "All right?"

"She's fine!" Paul read the meaning I couldn't voice.

My heart leaped. Shemyiah was all right! She was fine! What more could I ask?

Breathlessly, I listened while Paul filled in the details. "We were all eating dinner and watching the news on TV," Paul explained. "Then all of a sudden here comes this story about sheriffs finding five kids under a chicken coop in Lancaster. On a chicken ranch!"

It wasn't coming through fast enough for me. "What then?"

Paul grinned, enjoying filling us in on what had to be the biggest news we'd ever heard. "Well," he said, "it turned out they were 'Manson Family' kids. Sandy Good identified them. Said Dennis Rice was the father. Except one."

"Shemyiah!" I breathed.

"Right!" Paul confirmed. "Sandy claimed the youngest child — and she even called her Shemyiah — was given to the 'Family' about a year ago. She said they didn't know the parents' names!"

I looked at Erutan, then hit him on the shoulder. I couldn't contain my exuberance. "Isn't that neat?" I asked him. "They found Shemyiah!"

Erutan remained his usual reserved self. There was a hint of a smile, but nothing like the excitement I couldn't hold back.

I couldn't stand it. "How come you're not excited?" I asked him. "Oh, I am." But I knew better. He'd have shown it if he was.

Paul filled in some more details then. Shemyiah had been naked, hiding in a hole under a chicken coop with the other kids. There were guns and dope found, as well as the children. And they hadn't been able to identify my nine-and-a-half-month-old baby! The other extra youngster, I realized, was probably Moondog, who had not been with us at the cave.

"That's when I took off!" Paul went on. "We've been driving all night!"

I couldn't say anything at that point. I just grabbed my wonderful brother and hugged him. It was all I could do.

Then I looked at Erutan again. I'd made up my mind. "I'm splittin', man!" I said to him. "You comin', Erutan?"

He looked at me for a moment in that familiar deliberate fashion. A slight nod, and I knew I'd have help carrying out what I wanted to take from the cave. As far as I was concerned, this was it. I wanted my baby. I'd have to find some place where I could live till I could claim her. It couldn't be in a cave in the desert.

We gathered up our stuff, rolling it into packs for the trip. As we trailed down the hill toward the road where Paul and his friend had left their car, Paul reminded me of his earlier statement. "Don't you see?" he said. "Jesus is showing you!"

I nodded, not really caring how it had all come about. I was too excited knowing that Shemyiah was alive and all right to care about anything else. So it was easy to agree and let it go at that. I didn't really give it much thought, but I did flash for an instant on the possibility that he could be right...only for an instant. But a seed was planted.

Home and my parents were something I didn't feel like facing at that point. I couldn't help feeling guilty about having let Shemyiah go with the Family in the first place. When we reached Los Angeles at mid-morning, I asked Paul to take us to the Echo Park section where I'd be close to downtown. I had no idea what would come when I went to reclaim Shemyiah, but I wanted to be close to Civic Center, where I was sure I'd have to spend some time.

The place we chose was sort of a hippie district, containing the

"Brotherhood Village" — the big thing at the time was to follow Timothy Leary. I had to hock my flute to get twenty-five dollars to add to what cash we had left, to make up the fifty dollars for a month's rent. The place was on a hillside, with a hundred steps leading up to it — quite a climb. I noted with some degree of satisfaction that there was a Krishna Temple at the bottom of the hill. I could renew my old ties with that phase of religion if I felt it necessary.

My inquiries led me to MacLaren Hall in nearby El Monte, and when I identified myself as the mother of the baby named Shemyiah — the newspaper reports in the July 3, 1971, *Los Angeles Times* had spelled it 'Shamaya' — I met with skeptical looks.

"How do we know you're the mother?" I was asked. "How do we know you're not going to just take her out to the desert?" The matron-type lady shook her head. "You're a member of the Manson Family," she said then. "We don't believe you!"

My heart sank. How could I prove I was Shemyiah's mother? My eyes filled with tears. Then, more words. "How can we know for sure she's your daughter?"

I tried to stem the tears. I hadn't anticipated all this difficulty, although I'd realized it wasn't going to be any cut and dried situation. What could I say?

"You know, she's a very strange baby," the matron said then. "She doesn't cry — never. She doesn't fuss." A shake of the graying head. "Very strange."

I nodded, trying to smile, wishing I could come up with words that would convince this official that my baby was really mine. I thought back to something Mary had told me on that unexpected midnight visit, months before.

"She stopped crying after two weeks," Mary said. "Just like that."

And I thought, "Wow!" at the time. "They've really unprogrammed her!" It had blown my mind, and now, here it was again. A baby who didn't cry, didn't fuss, ever! I didn't know at the time that most babies are fussy until around three months old.

Then came the words I'd hoped for. "I guess you can see her now."

"Oh, thank you!" The words bubbled out before I could even think. I could see my baby again!

The matron disappeared, to come back a couple of minutes later with a baby girl in her arms. Yes! It was Shemyiah. Bigger — she'd grown, although not a lot. The same round, cherubic face. The same beautiful blue eyes. The same blond hair — more of it, now. And a strange sort of blank smile on her face. I took her, held her close, and again the tears trickled down my own face. My baby — safe and sound and in my arms!

But it wasn't to last. "We'll have to put her in a foster home," the matron said matter-of-factly. "You'll have to prove you can be a fit mother to her before we can ever give her back to you."

I nodded. I could sense a ray of hope in what she said. Her first remarks had questioned my even being the baby's mother; now she was, I felt, acknowledging that I was the mother. I'd simply have to prove I was fit for that responsibility.

Reluctantly, I left Shemyiah with the matron — no crying, no fuss, just that blank smile of acceptance from my baby. It didn't matter; I cried enough for both of us as I walked away from MacLaren Hall.

Much as I hated to admit I needed help, I felt I had no choice at this point. I knew I could not rely on my husband to come through, and I also knew one person who'd thought Shemyiah was something super-special. So I told Paul where I wanted to go, and he nodded, probably sharing my feeling that it was time to turn to Mom.

"We'll get a lawyer," she said determinedly after I laid out the details of my visit to the juvenile hall facility. "I'll get ready."

In the first law office we visited, the young attorney shook his head. "Sorry, we don't take cases like yours," he said. "But I'll give you the name of another lawyer who might be able to help."

He wrote down a name and address, and we wasted no time in visiting the second law office. Here the attorney, an older man, took us into a room where we sat down, and Mom explained our predicament.

"Now, young lady!" The lawyer fastened steely eyes on me. "Let's talk about your situation!"

I don't wish to recall the questions that followed. It was apparent from the first that this lawyer had no use whatsoever for the life-style I'd adopted. He was really uptight with me, right from the first. "Maybe if you changed, you might be a little

happier," he said at one point. By then, I didn't care what he said.
It was obvious this lawyer would be of less than no use to us.

"Maybe we ought to think it over," Mom said when we left the
office, and I nodded. Like her, I'd had enough of lawyers for one
day.

I went back to our hillside apartment, and to my surprise, a pair
of visitors showed up a short while later.

"Heard you were over here," was the greeting from T.J., the
Terrible, one of the first Family members I'd met. With him,
paired up as they'd often been when we were living with the
Family, was Bo.

And before our conversation had gone very far, T.J. had an
explanation. "Yeah," he said, "we split. The girls were getting
really weird, so we split."

I could imagine. The Manson trial, according to the papers and
radio reports, was still going on, with Family members remaining
near the steps of the Los Angeles Hall of Justice. I could well
imagine how weird the girls must be by now.

So we shared some pot and some reminiscences with T.J. and
Bo, and it was like old times. But I couldn't keep my mind off my
daughter. How was I to get her back?

Without really knowing why — I certainly couldn't have
expected to learn anything worthwhile from them — I went to visit
the girls camped at the Hall of Justice. "Hey, you know they found
Shemyiah," I said after greetings had been exchanged. "But I can't
get her back."

Squeaky just nodded knowingly, not saying anything, but
Brenda wasn't ready to accept that situation. "Just rip 'er off and
take her to the desert!" she advised. But I knew that wouldn't
work, so I just chatted, and then took my leave. But before I went,
I found that Country Sue and Kitty, both Family members, had
rented a place in the Silverlake district, between Echo Park where
we were and Hollywood. The other girls, I learned, would go
there to clean up and to stash their clothes and stuff, just like they
had in Duarte in earlier days.

And I saw something else, too. The girls were busy, as usual,
embroidering on some jackets, and when I chanced to glance
down, I could see big black and red letters spelling out "Devil's
Witches." I thought to myself, "How come you guys are putting

that on your jackets?" My thoughts must have shown on my face,
for Squeaky came up with an answer without my voicing the
question.

"Well," she said in those high-pitched little girl tones, "that's
what they want to hear — so that's what we're gonna do!" Weird!

Only a short time later, on August 21, 1971, Gypsy and Mary and
four of the male Family members raided an army surplus store in
Hawthorne, near Los Angeles International Airport, in hopes of
highjacking a ready-to-leave 747, after which they'd pose the
threat to kill one passenger in the plane each hour until Charles
Manson and all the other imprisoned Family members were
released. It was a bizarre scheme, of course — one that could
never have succeeded, I'm sure, and all it got was jail terms for
those participating. But from conversations I'd heard before, and
some that came after that when Erutan and I visited Country Sue's
apartment in the Silverlake district, it apparently was not the
first time the group had raided a surplus store to pick up guns
and other supplies. It was just that this time, they got caught,
perhaps because of the nature of their follow-up plans.

Anyway, we did go to Sue's shortly after that incident got a big
play in the papers, and from the time we arrived, I could see
Country Sue scheming on Erutan. Squeaky had stayed at the
corner downtown, but the others were there. We'd been there only
a short time when it bacame evident they were planning a venture
of a different nature.

My husband got the picture quickly, and turned to me. "Why
don't you go, too?" he asked. "We could use some bread!"

I shook my head. I didn't dig the idea of being a hooker, bread
or no bread.

"Oh, come on, Onjya," Sandy said then. "There's nothing
wrong with it. It's all just love."

"Sure," Sue said, with a come-on smile at my husband. "It's the
only way to go."

Reluctantly — and more because I wanted to keep an eye on Sue
than anything else — I agreed, and almost before I knew it, we
were out on the street in the Beverly Hills area. What happened
after that, I'm not entirely sure. I guess I must have blocked it out
of my conscious memory. Somehow, I do recall, we split up and
somewhere along the way, I remember sleeping with a couple of

guys, but I also remember that I didn't get any money for it. Whether that was due to my own inexperience as a prostitute, or for some other reason, I do not know. I just recall that I didn't dig it, and that I felt again the total inadequacy that had been my lot in life from the beginning. I couldn't even play the hooker role properly!

My husband, however, wasn't dismayed. He felt he'd suddenly discovered something important — a way for me to bring in the bread. "It's lots easier for you!" he declared. "I don't have any decent clothes to go get a job."

I pointed out that I didn't have any clothes, either — especially the kind I'd need for this sort of thing.

"You can borrow them from the Family," he argued. "I'll go get them for you."

I should have suspected then what was afoot. Sure enough, he did find some decent clothes for me, and I made an attempt at following the profession my husband wanted to push me into. But I didn't really know how to go about it. I was just walking the streets, and now and then asking people I saw where I might find some guys. I was getting less than nowhere. It finally dawned on me — hustling simply wasn't my dish. So I walked into a bar at Seventh and Alvarado and applied for a job as a topless dancer.

The manager looked me over. "Okay, let's see 'em!" he said. I slowly took off my blouse, wondering what would come next.

But he was coldly business-like. "Okay, you'll do," he announced. "Be here tonight — six o'clock."

And so the job began, and it wasn't really so bad. It was certainly better than hooking. The worst of it was, I'd have to hitchhike back to that hillside apartment at two in the morning, unless I could find someone at the bar who was interested enough to drop me off — and their interests were usually in another direction.

There was only one way to put up with that weird stripper's existence, and that was to stay on speed. It was easily available, at the bar, or anywhere near there. And I started taking it steadily; it was the only way I could live with myself. Always gnawing in the back of my mind were the words of the matron at MacLaren Hall, "You'll have to prove you can be a fit mother..." It seemed unlikely that my present position would offer much promise.

It didn't help, either, when I returned to the apartment one night to find Country Sue and Erutan in bed together. They made no effort to change the situation. Right there in my presence, with me in an adjoining bed, those two spent the night, while my stomach turned flip-flops and refused to let me sleep.

I'd disliked Country Sue from the first time I'd seen her; she reminded me of an evil rattlesnake. Now, my dislike was confirmed, intensified. I felt the urge to murder, deep within me, yet I knew that would solve nothing. I lay there condemning first my errant husband, then his floozy partner, while the night wore on.

My heart was filled with hate. I couldn't help it. After all we'd been through together...and now this, including the capping insult of flagrant disregard for me.

When morning came, Sue skipped out, leaving the two of us together. Erutan just sat and looked at me, guilt clouding his features. I knew he could easily see how uptight I was.

"You know, Onjya," he finally said quietly, "its beautiful. It's not wrong. I love her, she loves me, I love everybody."

I put in a few choice words that aren't fit to repeat.

"You don't mean anything more to me than she does," my husband said then. "I love her just as much as I love you."

That did it. I cursed him out with every hateful expression I could think of — a torrent of tongue-lashing. And I flounced out the door, unable to stand the sight of him another second.

"I'm sorry you feel that way, Onjya." His words echoed after me. Sorry indeed!

I didn't leave just to get away from my devious husband. I had to have some speed. I'd taken my last pill in the wee hours of morning, trying to ignore what was going on next to me. I had to have more speed — and quick!

By the time I got back, I had cooled off some, and despite the fact that I was high on speed, I was able to think clearly. When my husband began trying to kiss up to me, I began to see things squarely for the first time. It was just like a new light suddenly coming into my life, and I saw our situation as I'd never seen it before. It occurred to me, and for the first time, that if he wasn't guilty of a terrible misdeed, if it was all so right — then why did he look so guilty? I hadn't yet crystallized on a course of action, but I knew one thing: something had to give, and I wasn't sure it was going to be Onjya this time!

Then, one of those unexpected knocks at the door, and the minute I opened it, my heart sank. The identification the two well-dressed men held said it all — *FBI*. I shuddered.

Words formed in my mind. "I'm going to get busted for murder!" I said to myself in that brief instant. "I know it! I'll get busted for murder and that's going to be it!" The fact that I hadn't murdered anyone — although I had given it serious consideration — didn't occur to me.

Their questions were brief and to the point. They knew we were part of the Family; it seemed the Family had been trying to influence one young fellow, who was not yet twenty-one, to join. What did we know about it?

Actually, we knew nothing, beyond normal Family techniques used to recruit new members. Forgetting our previous differences of the day, Erutan and I leveled with the lawmen. Shortly they left.

But the FBI visit didn't clear up the other problem, the one my husband and I faced about our own relationship. I saw him now as being no good — no good whatsoever — for me. And though I wanted to do something about it, I wasn't sure what I should — or could — do. So I simply went back to the bar and did my nightly stint. In some ways, I thought, the situation was good. This way, I could be unattached — no ties to bind me if I wanted to go a separate way, and I could get into my work more wholeheartedly. But it was only speed that really kept me going. I was hooked. It was as simple as that!

This time it was I — not my husband — who made the decision that although we shared the same apartment, we were no longer man and wife. I would have none of him. And the desperation that accompanied this plight kept me from eating; I'd drink beer, because it could mix with speed — no problems; I couldn't drink anything stronger. I was chain smoking, of course. My shattered nerves kept me at that. In every way, it was a bummer.

Weeks went by, turning into months. I'd visited Shemyiah frequently at first, but as I began losing weight and was more and more jumpy from the speed I was taking steadily, I knew I would do my cause less than good if I showed up in that condition, so I began to avoid that trip, much as I wanted to see my daughter.

One Saturday morning when I woke up around eleven I sensed from the very moment I opened my eyes that Erutan was scheming again. It was a beautiful day outside, and I saw him looking out at a girl sitting on the hill with another guy.

"What are you looking out there for?" I asked.

"Oh, nothing. Just looking out."

But later on, he wandered down the hillside to where the girl, now alone, was sitting with her dog. I watched out the window. I could tell, just the way they acted, that he was up to something as he stroked the dog, smiling. I could just hear him, knowing from experience that he'd be saying, "Come on over. Have some grass. Let's get loaded." I didn't even have to be near them to hear him say it.

When I got home from work about three the next morning, there was a note from my husband. "I'm spending the night downstairs," I read. "I'll see you in the morning. I want to be with you tomorrow. I love you. Erutan."

That did it! Without thinking how it might sound to anyone else living in the apartments, I threw all of my husband's gear I could find down the steps leading to our place — his conga drums, sleeping bag, everything! I knew what would happen, and sure enough, in less than a week he was knocking at my door.

"Hey, Ilona won't let me stay any longer!"

"So what?" I said.

"Can I — move back in with you?" The tears in his eyes didn't fool me.

"Let me think about it!" I snapped.

Dropping his head in apparent shame, Erutan turned and started down the steps. Seeing his retreating figure, I suddenly saw red. I stepped to the side of the long stairway, picked up a rock, and without even thinking, threw it at my husband. It hit the back of his head; he stumbled, managed to stay on his feet, and rubbing his head with his hand, turned back up to me.

"Hey! You could have killed me!"

"I wish I had!" I breathed, turning to go back into the house. Then, because I was basically weak, I spoke further.

"I guess you can come back. You can stay, but not as my husband!"

He looked at me, nodded, and moved on down to gather up his gear. It had been some time since he'd been accepted in that apartment as a husband, so it really wasn't any big change. It was just that everything was out in the open now. There would be no pretense whatsoever. I would not let him touch me.

What followed came in such rapid succession it is difficult to recall, especially since I was high on speed on an almost continuous basis. First, one of the guys who came often to the bar began to pick up on me, and I started going out with him. At 34, and married, he was more of a father image than anything else, but I imagined myself to be in love with him. He kept telling me things about my husband — things I'd never actually pinned down.

"He's been using you all this time!" Bill would say. "It's no good, Onjya, no good!" Down deep, I knew he was right. But what was I to do?

That was one development. The second one was even more profound. My mother obtained custody of Shemyiah. How she managed it, I'm not sure, but it happened. I could see my daughter now, occasionally, with no hassle beyond the always difficult situation at home. It made no difference to Erutan; he'd refused to go see Shemyiah when she was at MacLaren; now he refused to see her at my folks' home in La Puente.

The third development was devastating. It came shortly after Christmas, a normally happy time when I'd visited my baby, only to be confronted with some scathing remarks by my mother.

"You look like you're doing to die!" she announced, as usual, pulling no punches. I knew what she meant; my face was sunken in, my eyes burned in their sockets. I was so thin my clothes hung loose no matter how I tried to tighten them. I was just rotting away, turning to a vegetable.

Mom kept staring at me. "You're gonna die! Are you on drugs and stuff?"

"No," I said innocently. "Huh-uh!"

But the speed was getting to me, no question. For once, I almost agreed with my mother. I actually felt like I was going to die. I was glad when the Christmas bit was over, so I could cop some more speed.

The third development, which I mentioned, came when I went back to work. As trashy as that place was, the owner fired me on the spot. "I'm doing this because I think it'll do you good!" he told me, and I knew he meant it. "You're just too thin. You've got to come down off whatever it is you're tripping out on."

I didn't much care, I told myself. Onjya Sipe — the girl who'd failed at everything else — was now a failure at topless dancing. I couldn't even hold a job in a bar!

More days dragged by while I stayed high on speed. Then, the kidney infection set in, and an angry lump raised over my right hip. Erutan paid no attention; he'd stayed in a marijuana fog from the time I'd said he could return to the apartment — but not as my husband.

And so came the time when I could stand it no longer. I knew my mom was right. I was going to die. I could feel the presence of that grim messenger outside the door, and I wanted no part of him — yet.

So I dialed Paul, and I told him I was putting down, needed to go to the hospital, and could he come and get me.

"I'll be right over!" Never were four words more welcome.

I thought back over the troubled route that had brought me to this desperate point in my life. I'd called my friend, Bill, for a long chat before I'd called Paul. But it hadn't helped. My mind had blanked out the minute I hung up; I couldn't remember a word he'd said.

"I don't care if I get busted," I said aloud to myself now. "I don't care what happens!" And I didn't.

Somehow, I survived the pain until Paul arrived. It wasn't easy. I'd filled another ash tray, and was stretched out on the floor when he came. I managed to sit up, but I couldn't muster strength enough to stand.

"JoAnn!" His voice was confident, full of authority. "Jesus can heal you right now! Why don't you give Him a chance?"

I hesitated. What good could that possibly do? But on the other hand — what harm? If Paul thought...

"You've tried everything else," Paul put in then. "Just give Jesus a chance!"

A spasm of pain sliced across my lower back. I closed my eyes. Suddenly I realized this emptiness inside. It was putrid.

"Okay," I said weakly. "I'll try it. What do I do?"

16

A New Life —
In Christ!

My brother looked deep into my eyes, and looking back at him, I sensed a power there that was far above and beyond his own limited years. It was not the power vibe I'd felt at times with the Manson Family. It was stronger, heavier, more all-encompassing. I waited, wondering what unseen force was present there in that room.

"First of all, you need God to heal you," Paul said quietly, yet confidently. "Just let me pray for you."

He laid his hands on me, and as he prayed, I could feel a new strength flow into my tortured body. I could actually feel the spirit of God flooding into me — a whole new life — and I hadn't even asked the Lord to come into my heart! He just came in anyway, touching me by His spirit.

I stood up, something I hadn't been able to do only a few minutes before. Suddenly, the drowning effects of the speed I craved were gone. The pain of the kidney infection disappeared; I felt, literally, like a new person. And it was more than I could take.

"Wow!" I said. "What's going on?" All this overwhelming spirit of love, this new life, this total change of outlook was too much for me. I couldn't believe it!

Paul looked at me again in that thoughtful way that seemed to hold so much unseen power. "Do you want to accept Jesus in your heart now?" he asked.

The power of God which had already filled me left no room for doubt. "Yeah!" I said eagerly. But it was all so new. I didn't know what to do, what came next. So I said, "But I don't know how to pray!"

Paul nodded. "Just repeat this prayer," he told me, "BUT believe it with all your heart!"

Paul laid his hand on my shoulder again, and I repeated his words, really believing them as I prayed after him.

"Jesus, forgive me for my sins. I confess I am a sinner. I believe that You died for me and rose from the dead again."

As before, I could feel a surge of power within that room, as I repeated those significant words.

Paul went on. "I open my heart to You and ask You to come in." Again I repeated his words, and the minute I said them, I could super-feel that the force in that place was ever-so-much more real than even I was! The love of God just came in and filled my heart and soul and it was just a perfect fit, in every way!

I began to cry. "I don't even feel like I've taken speed!" I told my brother. "I just feel brand new — like a baby! I feel like pure gold!"

Paul nodded, a smile of joy beaming from his face. "Praise God!" he said.

I suddenly realized what I'd just said, realized that the words had come not from me, but from the righteousness of Jesus Christ that had filled my heart, soul, and body.

"Praise God!" I repeated. And then, reverting to my more normal character, I almost drew back my fist to slug my wonderful brother.

"Man!" I said, "Why didn't you tell me about Jesus sooner?"

Just realizing that Jesus was real, that He held such boundless power was blowing my mind.

Paul grinned. "I was trying to tell you," he reminded me, "but Satan had you bound! Now you see the light!"

I stood there in bewilderment. It was all just too much. "Jesus Christ?" I repeated the name, wondering at its total beauty. He was real. He was really alive...yet He had died on the cross to bring life everlasting to the rest of us. I'd heard about Him, but only briefly. I knew He was the one they preached about in the churches, but I'd never paid much attention to Him or what He meant. Yet, now, He wasn't at all the way I'd thought He was. He was so neat, so really beautiful, so glorious! He was Jesus Christ, the Lord of all!

"I can't believe how perfect He fits!" I said then, unable to contain my enthusiasm. "I can just feel every detail of it, the way God has moved in." And then I remembered that Paul and I were not alone in that room.

"Erutan, man!" I turned to my husband. "Accept the Lord in YOUR heart. He's — marvelous!"

Erutan shrugged. "Okay," he said without enthusiasm. "What do I do?"

Paul put his hand on my husband's shoulder and again repeated the prayer, with Erutan mumbling it after him. When they were through, my husband shrugged his shoulders again.

"So nothing happened!" he said, "What now?"

Paul nodded. "Sometimes," he said quietly, "you don't feel anything. You have to believe!"

I was sure I knew why Erutan didn't feel anything. He had simply mouthed the words; his heart was still a slave to Satan. And I knew, in that instant, what I had to do, for deep within, I could hear a new voice guiding my footsteps, giving me strength.

"Leave everything behind, Onjya," it said. "Don't look back. Go!"

I didn't hesitate. I began gathering up my skimpy belongings. I knew where that voice came from, and I knew it was, at long last, the truth I'd searched for all my life.

"What'cha doin'?" The usual disinterest clouded my husband's voice.

"I'm going with Paul," I announced. "Paul, help me get this stuff together."

It didn't take long. We started down the steps, and I could hear my husband's complaining tones echoing behind me.

"I don't see why you have to take off," he was saying. "You hadn't ought to do that!"

Paul put his free hand — his other one held a battered suitcase — on my shoulder. "Do you really want to leave him?" he asked.

I knew what I had to do. "Yeah!" I said emphatically. "I have to!"

And then, moving down that long series of steps, I bubbled over with the new exuberance I'd felt ever since my burden of sin was lifted. "Paul!" I said. "I feel just like I'm floating down these stairs!"

"That's the way it is!" Paul confirmed. "You know you've made your decision for Jesus!"

And so began a new chapter in my life. At home, there was the usual reserve in accepting me — suspicious looks that I couldn't really blame Mom and Dad for casting in my direction. After all, my track record there and elsewhere left a few things to be desired. But with my new-found outlook of peace instead of war, I did my best to gain approval instead of rejection.

Despite Paul's urgings, I refused at first to go to church with him. "I have to grow in the Lord," I told him. "I'm not ready for that yet."

I dug in on the Bible I found at home, reading it at every opportunity. But I knew I'd have to do my part for the family if I was to remain at home, so when my aunt suggested she might be able to help me get a job, I jumped at the chance. It was factory work, operating a machine to make plastic tops for lotion bottles. While I tried to keep my attention on the work I was doing, I often found my mind filled with wondering what the Lord had in store for me. And I wondered, too, what course of action I should take concerning some personal matters.

For one, I was still going out with Joe, another man whom I'd met while working at the bar. He had a certain charm that I really dug, and I felt I was in love with him. I had no wish to get back on the speed that had sustained me for so long. However, Joe was a bar-hopper, and I drank along with him, burying in the back of my mind the knowledge that what I was doing was not what the Lord wanted me to do.

A second problem was my husband, who called the house frequently at first. He would cry and go on to Mom, and because I refused to talk to him, he'd carry on something fierce about how he needed me back. "I didn't realize what I had," he'd complain. It gave me the chance to analyze what had happened over the years, and I knew that phase of my life was over.

"We can begin again," Erutan told my mother at one point. "We'll go to Hawaii and grow avocados."

"That's just the trouble," I explained to Mom afterwards. "He's always got a big dream. 'I'll write a book, I'll do this, and I'll do that.' But nothing ever happens."

"You're the one who picked him out," Mom reminded me.

I agreed. "That's right," I said, "and it was a mistake from the first. He's just out of touch with reality. He's in one world and I'm in another."

My mother gave me that sharp, penetrating look that was part of her personality. "I hope you know what you're saying," she said.

I nodded. "I do!" I said. "He was only security in the first place. And I have a new kind of security now." I didn't bother to point out that I meant security in the Lord. "And I just don't have any more love for him — none at all!"

Mom nodded, apparently satisfied. We didn't often agree, but this seemed to be an occasion when we did. By this time, there was another problem between us — one that I wasn't sure we'd ever be able to resolve. Mom, as I've already mentioned, managed through some kind of finagling to obtain custody of my daughter, Shemyiah. So it was a situation where I had my daughter — and yet I didn't have her, for Mom was almost immediately off on a "trip" concerning the baby. Shemyiah, as far as Mom was concerned, was hers. I might as well have been a perfect stranger.

I wanted to be a real mother to my daughter, but my own mother was so deep into the motherhood bit, I didn't have a chance. I began to wonder if I'd ever have the opportunity to prove I was a fit mother — the requirement expressed previously by the juvenile authorities when the baby was first found.

So my life, despite the new freedom I'd found in accepting Jesus Christ, was still filled with problems, and none of them was easy to solve. I finally decided that perhaps Paul's continued urging that I go to church with him would offer a partial solution; at least, I felt, it would possibly broaden my outlook, and strengthen my faith in the Lord.

But within minutes after I set foot in the church building, I freaked out. My nervous fear of the unknown apparently triggered an acid flashback, and I was once again under satanic control. I turned and without a word, ran from the church, taking refuge in my brother's car. He and his girl friend where there almost immediately.

"JoAnn!" Paul said anxiously. "What happened?"

"I — I don't know!" I said, unable to get out the words that would explain my problem. "I — I just can't go in there!"

Paul's perception, as usual, was remarkable. "It's just Satan influencing you," he analyzed. "Come on back, JoJo. We'll get the pastor and the others to pray for you."

That was more than I was ready for. With my meager experience in the Lord, I was frightened by the fine Christian people I saw in the church. Once again, as so many times in the past, I felt my own inadequacy. In a word, they scared me off.

To Paul, I said, "No, let's go home!" My flashback had frightened me more than I cared to admit. As secure as I'd felt in my new faith in Jesus Christ, it told me my problems were not all solved. And knowing it had happened the one time I'd decided to try going to church, I wanted no part of staying that day. Paul took me home.

I sought refuge in going out with Joe that same evening, under the impression that he loved me as I thought I loved him. Somewhere along the way, I had a suggestion.

"Let's get married!" I said. As simple as that. I don't know how I figured it could happen. I was still married to Chuck (Erutan) Sipe, and Joe himself was likewise matched.

"Good idea," Joe agreed. "We'll have to think about it."

His searching hands confirmed what I'd begun to suspect. Joe had no interest in me, beyond physical satisfaction. He was using me, taking advantage of my weaknesses, using much the same technique I'd witnessed in the Manson Family. He could make me feel like I really belonged, like I was accepted for what I was, but it was just a game with him — anything to get what he wanted, including playing on my distrust of my parents. I began to wonder again if I would ever get everything straightened out, even with my new-found faith. I hid in a dark corner of my mind the knowledge that I was being less than loyal to that faith in what I was doing now.

I even went so far as to talk with Joe's wife, with whom he was still living. She wasn't surprised. "He isn't about to leave me!" she announced after I'd introduced myself and explained why I had come. "I've been trying to get rid of him for years!"

It really hurt me, verifying my previous realization that I was being used. So that night, I started to tell him where it was at, and he began to get violent in his speech and actions. I knew there was a gun always handy — either on his person or in the glove compartment. I was suddenly frightened of what might happen. I took immediate refuge in my new-found faith.

"You know, Joe," I said, "I wonder just when Jesus is coming back." I paused, hoping that bringing the Lord into the picture would change the pattern of Joe's behavior. "He is coming back, you know."

Joe only grunted. I was aware that he was an ex-convict, and I could only hope he would not react unfavorably to my conversation. "You can't imagine how great it is to know Jesus is on your side," I said.

Another grunt, but I could sense that his violent nature had cooled somewhat. I also knew better than to bring up again the subject of our own future — together or otherwise.

But the conversation had been sufficiently notable for Joe to get the message that it was time I went home, and as we drove, I kept seeing a white light somewhere in front of me. Then came a voice, from deep within: "Follow the light!" And it was repeated: "Follow the light!" I said nothing about it to Joe, for I was sure he would not understand. I had the feeling that Jesus was talking to me, but I wasn't sure. I wasn't really close to the Lord yet, so I couldn't be certain the light and the words were coming from Him.

The next day, however, thinking about what had happened the night before, I was puzzled. I was hanging clothes on the line, and I suddenly decided it was time to check some things out with God. If He was really on my side, I felt, He would come up with some answers.

So I said it out loud: "There's just not one person I can trust!" I was forgetting my brother, of course; I was really thinking about Joe, with whom I'd thought I was in love.

The answer came to me clear and quick: "You can trust me!" I knew it was Jesus, speaking directly to me.

I shook my head. "Wow!" My experiences were becoming more and more startling all the time.

Later that day, my brother handed me a tract explaining the Rapture when Christ will come in the sky and remove His people from earth. Then great troubles will break out in the world. When

I read it, I decided more firmly than ever that I wanted to dedicate my life to Christ. When I went to bed, it was to dream — and then to dream again.

At first, I kept hearing the voice of Jesus. "I love you!" He said to me. As suddenly as He had come, He was gone, only to return shortly and tell me, "Remember — I'm coming soon!" I awoke, thinking about the Rapture report I'd read. Then I slept again, again to dream.

This time I thought I was going down a freeway in a car, with a big truck ahead. Suddenly, I could feel all this goodness around us; then it all changed and I realized that all the Christians were gone. The Rapture had happened, and the spirit of God was gone. And I knew that there was only wickedness in me, that I was no good at all. I had the feeling, "I'm in hell. I'm going to hell!" I awoke in a cold sweat, keenly aware of my sins, fearful that I was too late.

Frightened, I awakened Paul, to tell him what I had dreamed. He nodded, a reassuring smile on his lips. "That's Jesus speaking to you through your dreams," he told me. "He really wants you to give Him your life, JoAnn. He sometimes does this — speaks to people in dreams and visions." When I was fully awake I realized my sins had already been forgiven when I received Jesus, but now I was amazed. He wanted my life.

And I thought, "Wow! That's far out!" But it gave me a lot of new hope. If the Lord saw fit to speak to me through my dreams, He had to be real, and it was up to me to listen to Him. I thought back over my experiences of the past few days — the shining light, the voice, the dreams.

"If this is the real thing, man, I want to get into it!" I declared to myself. I was sure now I'd found the truth. I tried to look at it from every angle, and it held up all the way. "This," I thought, "has got to be it — the truth at last!" I knew, yet I'm not sure I fully realized it even then, that I'd finally bridged that final inch. I'd felt so many times before that I was on the verge of full enlightenment, that I was almost in touch with the true reality of life. Now, in Christ, the pages of life's mysterious book had finally opened to me.

On a Sunday morning, I was preparing to go out with Joe once more when Paul confronted me. "Why don't you come to church?" he asked.

"I will, Paul," I said. "I will." In the back of my mind was the knowledge that I hadn't said when I'd do it. I felt this let me out of an immediate commitment. I kept on getting ready for the date with Joe. I'm sure Paul realized what was going on.

"Man," he said, "Jesus would really dig it. If you loved Him as much as you're faithful to one guy when you like him — you give everything you have!" He shook his head, a little sadly. "If you'd only do that with Jesus — wow!"

I went on the date with Joe, but my brother's words echoed in my ears, along with my own promise concerning going to church. "I will! I will!" And suddenly, I knew what I had to do.

"Joe," I said, "please stop the car."

He pulled to the curb without a word. "Joe, I promised Paul I'd go to church with him," I said. "I think I'd better keep that promise. Will you take me home?"

Joe looked at me questioningly for a moment, then started the car and turned back the way we had come. "This Jesus bit is really getting to you, isn't it?" he said.

"Jesus is real! I love him!" I said simply. "And He loves you — and me!"

Joe nodded. "Well," he said, "I respect you for keeping your promise to your brother." And as we drove up to the house, "I'll see you later."

I did see Joe later — only once more, for a very brief time. And when I went to church that day, there was none of the freaked-out fear that had chased me away the first time. I still found it hard to talk to people. I was shaking inside, but I stood my ground and didn't run away. More than once, I breathed three words to myself, "Help me, Jesus!" And it worked.

Paul was due to spend the afternoon at a friend's house that day, and as he dropped me off at our house, he laid some meaningful words on me.

"I guess you're going to have to decide who you love more — Jesus or Joe," he said. "I hope you make the right decision."

He left, and I was alone with my thoughts. In my room, I got on my knees and prayed. As I did, final conviction seemed to come to my mind and my mouth. "Wow!" I said out loud to myself. "I know now what I want!"

I couldn't wait. I dialed Paul's friend and got my brother on the telephone. "Paul!" I said. "I've decided! I want to love Jesus more! I want to surrender my whole life to Him!"

My brother's voice was firm and clear, as always, "Praise God!" he said. "You've really come to the Lord at last!"

17

Secure —
In the Lord!

I really meant it. I was ready to give my life to the Lord. Whatever problems I would face, I would look to the Lord for deliverance. It was a different feeling from anything I'd ever experienced. It was as though a load of a thousand years had been lifted from my heart. I was free at last! I thought back to a few days before, when I'd first realized Christ had unlocked the door to life for me. No question — this was it!

To Paul's surprise, I began attending the Christian Chapel in Walnut with him. I soon learned that worshipping regularly, and sharing my testimony of the power of Jesus Christ to forgive us our sins was an exhilarating experience.

Not long after that, I was fired from my job. I was too slow, they said. Maybe they were right. I'll admit that my mind was on my new-found faith more than it was on keeping up with the machines that turned out plastic bottles. But it didn't really bother me; months before, a blow like that would have been devastating, a put-down that my ego would have tried to scorn, with disastrous results. But as it was, I accepted getting sacked as part of the Lord's will. I knew He had a place for me, and I just said, "God wants me to go to church more."

So I bent every effort to grow in the Lord, taking every opportunity for fellowship with other Christians, sharing my testimony at every available occasion. I found that those around me were eager to hear of my experiences, that the knowledge that God had put me to the test and had brought me back to His fold held promise for even the lowest offender.

It was my brother, Paul, who baptized me — a meaningful immersion that I felt cleansed my soul of the grief that had plagued it for so long. Yet, before the true baptism of the Holy Spirit was realized, there were still problems to be reckoned with... problems that held over from my disordered past.

Sin, in all its many forms, is something all of us have to face up to. Despite my profession of faith in the Lord, and my sincere acceptance of Him as the true answer to all the problems of humanity, there was one particular habit I couldn't face giving up, until it came to me in prayer that I was still allowing sin to play a definite part in my life. A sin can be a little thing, I found. You keep doing it, and it doesn't seem so very bad, so you close your eyes to the reality of it. A little white lie now and then, perhaps; some other action you know, down deep, is done without the Lord's approval; in my case it was cigarettes.

Not pot — I'd cast that aside when I left Chuck (Erutan) Sipe. Tobacco. For some, it may be that cigarettes or other tobacco use is not necessarily a sin, and I do not mean to condemn those who view it otherwise. But for Onjya Sipe, the Lord God revealed to me that this was something that had to be eliminated from my life, and what a struggle that was!

I'd been a chain smoker. It was an automatic action to reach for a cigarette — frequently. When I accepted Jesus Christ in my life, I thought nothing of this situation at first. Gradually, the Lord revealed to me that it was wrong for me to smoke. At first, I merely stopped smoking in public. I didn't want to set a poor example for those around me. So I'd smoke at home and in private only. Then I realized that simply wasn't enough. I not only had to quit, I felt the hand of God on my shoulder. I could hear His voice telling me what I had to do.

So I'd stop smoking for a time, and I'd think I'd whipped the problem. The first thing I knew, I'd be back at the corner store buying a pack of cigarettes. I hated myself, because I knew I should have been sharing the joy of the Lord with the proprietor instead of buying smokes. And before I knew it, the Lord brought that up to me when I was praying to Him.

"You know when you go to the store," He said to me, "you know what you should be doing."

"Oh," I said. "You mean I have to go there and confess my sins?"

"No," the Lord told me then. "You don't have to at all, but if you want to get closer to me, here's your opportunity."

I gasped, realizing how important this really was. "Praise God!" I said then. "I'll do it!"

The very next morning, I really felt led by the Lord to carry through on my pledge, so I headed for the corner store, knowing I had to confess my sins before I would really be right with the Lord. I took my Bible in my hand for reassurance. I drove there, got out of the car, walked in, and looked at the storekeeper. He looked back and smiled.

"Hi!" I said. "Remember me?"

"Yes," he said. "I do. How are you?"

"Well, remember when I came in here — pretty often, I guess — and I bought cigarettes?"

"Yeah, I remember." There was a puzzled look on his face, and no wonder. He couldn't possibly have known what I was leading up to.

Then it all just gushed out. "Well, I'm a Christian," I said, holding up my Bible as evidence. "I really love the Lord and everything, and I've sinned against God and I've sinned against you, and the Bible says to confess your sins, and the Lord's just delivered me from smoking and it's really a struggle, but it's still sin."

I paused for a breath while the man just stood there, sort of puzzled-looking, slowly nodding his head as he listened. "I don't know what you're going to think of me," I went on. "You can kick me out of here or something if you want. But I'm really sorry. Would you forgive me?"

Still that puzzled look, another brief nod. "I should just share Jesus with you instead of buying cigarettes," I acknowledged. "I feel so bad that I haven't done it!"

And then the words came easier. "But I do want to tell you about Jesus," I went on. "Jesus really loves you, you know! He can really change your life and give you what you're seeking for. He's really done a lot in my life!"

A couple of other people had walked in the store, and were standing there watching us, obviously wondering, "What's going

on here?" But I didn't mind. I knew I had to do what I had to do. It
was the Lord's will.

About then, the storekeeper's face suddenly took on a new
expression, and I knew Jesus was putting the right words in my
heart and my mouth. "Would you like to accept the Lord?" I
asked.

The man looked me squarely in the eyes, and there was a
determination in his own eyes that made me realize I'd reached out
and touched his heart. "You know," he said, "I really think that's
what I need!"

Completely ignoring the other people in the store, I reached out
and grabbed his hand in both of mine. "Just repeat this prayer
after me," I told him, saying the same words Paul had said when I'd
made my own decision for Christ. And he repeated, out loud and
word for word, the prayer that came from my heart that morning,
and a new Christian was born.

It was so exciting I could hardly contain myself. That same day,
I brought him some Christian literature, and prayed with him
again. I invited him to share the inspiration of the Christian
Chapel, as Paul had done with me. And he did, attending regularly
after that and growing in the Lord along with the rest of us.

It was not until late that evening that I realized I had not only
brought a fellow human being to the supreme experience of
accepting the Lord in his heart, but I had also hurdled the obstacle
I'd set out to conquer. I had shared Jesus Christ instead of buying
more cigarettes. And not one time since has a cigarette touched my
lips!

There were other trials, too. Perhaps it is the way of the Lord
to test us out, to beset us with tribulations and with occasional
temptations, to give us the chance to prove to Him we really do
love and trust Him.

One of my biggest problems was trying to become a true mother
to my daughter, Shemyiah. The old conflicts with my own mother
were even more in evidence than they'd been many times in my
growing-up years. Now she had legal custody of my child, and she
had her own ideas about raising her.

So I'd take my eighteen-month-old baby with me whenever I
could get her away from the house, just to be able to share with her
the love and understanding that filled my heart. I wanted her to

come to know me as her mother, not as some stranger who was just around on the scene, but didn't really mean much to the youngster.

The Reverend George Crites, pastor of the Christian Chapel, had given me the opportunity to testify before others quite frequently. Because he was such a devout Christian himself, he gave extra effort to helping me make the Lord the key to my life. As a result, he gave me a car to drive, so I could get around more easily and not miss any opportunity to speak up for the Lord.

There came a day when I had no particular goal in mind, other than to spend some time alone with my daughter, so Shemyiah and I went for a ride. Noticing that we were low on gas, I stopped at a service station. While I was there, I decided to call about a part-time job I'd seen advertised in our local newspaper. I took Shemyiah to the phone booth with me to make the call. I was talking with the person about it when I saw three black-and-white cop-cruisers swarm up beside my own car.

"Praise God!" I thought to myself. "This is one time I don't have to worry about them coming for me. I sure didn't do anything wrong!" I answered a couple of more questions from the prospective employer.

About that time, Bang! Bang! Bang! A cop was knocking, in no uncertain terms, on the door of the telephone booth. I terminated the conversation as quickly as I could, picked up Shemyiah, and probably looking as puzzled as I felt, pulled open the door of the booth. Flashbacks of other days flooded over me, for cops had been very much a part of my life, from an early age. But now...

"Is this your car?" The policeman pointed toward the auto parked beside the gas pump.

"Yes," I said, "it is."

"You're under arrest!" Just like that! And before I could gather my wits to protest, he added two words. "Stolen car!"

I couldn't squeeze any words out of my astonished being, but the thoughts were there. "Oh, no! After all this time, I get busted for — but I didn't do it! I couldn't have!" And then, a paralyzing thought!

"Shemyiah!" I squeaked it out loud. "Can I drop her off somewhere?"

"Sure," one of the cops said. "We can arrange that."

So I knew, right then and there, that the Lord's hand was on my shoulder. And even while the cops were handcuffing me, in front of the daughter who I'd been trying to impress as being her very own mother, my mind was racing with a new challenge.

"You're gonna get it!" I was saying to myself, but addressing my thoughts to the cops. "I'm gonna witness to all you guys, and I'm gonna get Jesus Christ to touch every one of you!"

I explained that I wanted to leave Shemyiah with my mother. When they agreed and we got into their car, it finally dawned on me that I hadn't really explained the situation.

"Hey," I said, "about that car. My pastor gave it to me!"

One cop laughed out loud. "Now that's a good one!" he said. "That's about as likely as an airplane flapping its wings like a bird!"

"This is terrible!" I went on. "I'm a sincere Christian! I'm telling the truth!"

"Sure!" came the reply.

"Listen!" I said. "It's Jesus, man. You need Jesus Christ!"

And I went on talking about the Lord all the way to the station house. They couldn't shut me up. Once we were there, I shared a cell with a girl even younger than I was. I began talking to her about my faith and what it could do for her.

"Jesus doesn't want you to run away," I told her. "He wants to meet you right where you are — right here!" I pointed to the walls of the jail cell. "He's waiting — right now!"

I knew then the Lord had sent me to this place, because my new friend became a friend in Jesus, accepting Him then and there, just like I'd said. It seemed a miracle, for I knew I was being used of the Lord.

Shortly after that, Pastor George Crites arrived on the scene to help get things straightened out. At first he was as puzzled as I was, for one of the church members had given the car to George. When it was all checked out, the answer was fairly simple, however. The car had been stolen about four years before, and later returned to the owner, but not through the authorities. He'd forgotten to report its return so it was still on the records as a stolen car. When someone spotted it as I was driving by, they figured they had a car theft suspect for sure.

But I'd had the opportunity to witness to those cops, and I'd brought that girl to the Lord. She later came to my church, by the way. A frightening incident, possibly just another of the Lord's tests for Onjya, turned out to have fruitful results.

A few days later, I was driving along and a black-and-white drove up beside me. The uniformed driver motioned for me to pull over and stop, which I did — a sinking feeling enveloping my heart. "Not again!" I thought. "How long is this nonsense going to go on?"

But it turned out to be one of the policemen who'd escorted me to the station that day. "I just wanted to make sure everything was okay with you," he said with a smile. "I'm really sorry that we had to take you in the other day."

I was so relieved that two words just popped out. "Praise God!" I said, smiling back. "It all worked out for the best."

The cop nodded. It was almost as if he'd known all along that I wasn't really guilty. "Well," he said, "if there's anything we can ever do for you..." and he walked back to his car. I had the feeling I should have tried to tell him some more about Jesus Christ then and there, but I just wasn't thinking fast enough. The relief of not being arrested again was so heavy I couldn't get any other words out.

Everyone, I suppose, has problems, now and again. That's why it is such a wonderful relief to be able to take them to the Lord and through His loving care to bid them good-bye. My own problems in those months when I was constantly growing in the Lord and learning His marvelous ways were sometimes almost more than I could cope with. And I wasn't experienced enough as a sincere Christian to be able to take them where they belonged — to Him.

The adjustment to Christian life was not easy, of course; nor was it easy to stand by and see my daughter being brought up by my mother, with whom I'd disagreed much of the time since my own babyhood. So when I failed to find an understanding friend who had had experiences similar to mine in my church — someone I could pour out my heart to — I felt rejected, as I had most of my life until that time. I had faith that Jesus Christ would bring me through, yet I realized I wasn't always doing just what I should for Him, and I'd get down on myself, feeling I simply couldn't do it on my own.

It all led to one thing, of course. Satan would peer over my shoulder, and his words were a tempting whisper. "If you just took a little speed, Onjya, you'd have a lot more confidence in yourself. You need speed — remember?" It was almost as if I could hear an actual voice telling me those lies. "You're psychologically bound to speed, Onjya," the voice said. "You can't be you without it; you can't be a real human being without it. Better get some now!"

Lies! I knew they were lies! And yet...

And then I'd talk to myself. "You can't help it," I'd say. "Of course you can't do it all on your own. You don't even feel like a human being. You can't even talk to anybody. But some speed..."

I was almost out the door. I knew where I could lay hands on some speed, of course. But something held me back. I reached for the telephone. Maybe — just maybe — there was a way.

"Melodyland — Drug Prevention! May I help you?" The girl's voice on the telephone was so filled with confidence, with the spirit of the Lord, that I felt better just hearing those few words.

But it wasn't easy to talk about my problem. "I — I used to take speed," I said hesitantly. "I'm not taking now, but I..."

"You keep thinking how nice it would be to get back on it, don't you?"

"Yes," I said. "That's it! I'm a Christian, but I can't seem to..."

"Praise God!" interrupted the confident voice again. "You're a Christian, so you've already won the battle. Will you pray with me?"

"Oh, yes!" I exclaimed. "I need someone to pray with!"

"Dear Lord!" came the voice on the phone. "You know how you saved me from the drug scene, how you came into my heart and took me away from Satan's clutches forever!"

I sighed. I hadn't thought very much about others having the same problems I had. Apparently this girl had been there, along with me.

"Jesus, you know and I know there's no place for speed and such in the heart and life of a Christian! Lord, cleanse her heart. Give her strength. Let her know she's put that sort of thing behind her forever!"

I felt a new surge of confidence sweep over me. "Praise God!" I said. "I'll never touch it again!"

18

Miracles —
In the Faith!

Confidence in the Lord and His guidance had brought me through some major problems. It took me awhile to even realize how much was accomplished in this total turn-around from a life filled with problems to one overflowing with love, hope, and dedication to Christian principles.

In fact, I'm still realizing — every day — what a tremendous lot was done in my life with His coming. As my days of worship became more and more meaningful, I began to feel more and more the influence of the Holy Spirit, to the point where I finally had to bring it up to the Reverend George Crites.

"I want to be baptized in the Holy Spirit," I said. "What do I do?"

One of the church members was standing near-by with her daughter and overheard my request. George glanced at them and nodded, and the lady said, "Come on with us. We'll help you."

They led me to a small room at the rear of the church, where I sat down in a chair. The two of them explained how the Holy Spirit came to those who were ready for Him. I'd already felt the need, and I'd been filled with the Holy Spirit, but not to overflowing, as I knew I would have to be if I was to be baptized in the Spirit.

"Just picture Jesus laying His hands on you," were the next words I heard. At the same time, both the lady and her daughter laid their hands on me, starting to talk in language unfamiliar to me. It was, of course, speaking in tongues, and I marveled at the religious conviction which made such action possible.

Within only a few minutes, I could feel the Holy Spirit simply overflowing from me, and I couldn't help jumping up and hugging the two people who had brought me to this unique experience.

"I've got it! I've got it!" I shouted. It was neat, like walking into another dimension. "Thank you, Jesus!"

The room wasn't big enough to contain my enthusiasm. I burst out with the same words on my lips. "I've got it!" I yelled. "I've got it!"

"Hey, wait a minute!" someone said. "What'd you get?"

"You know!" I said. "The Spirit!"

George came up then, and I threw my arms around him, I was so overjoyed. "Wow!" he said with a happy smile. "Looks like you've really been baptized in the Holy Spirit!"

I went on bubbling, hugging everyone I could find, because I was so very happy at having been baptized in the Spirit.

"Hey," George said finally, "I'm going to have to send you out before you explode!"

"I'm ready!" I announced. "Praise God! It's wonderful!"

George was as good as his word. He made arrangements for me to appear at the Calvary Chapel in Costa Mesa, where there was a large fellowship with thousands of people gathered. Before that, at various times, I'd shared my testimony at small meetings with Mrs. Crites, but never before anywhere near such a large group.

But I leaned on the Lord, and as usual, He brought me through it. The Costa Mesa meeting was followed by a visit to Melodyland on a Tuesday night, when the young people usually went. I shared my testimony there, too, and afterward while we were getting ready to leave the parking lot, Ralph Wilkerson sent some people out to find me. Wilkerson pastors the Melodyland work in Anaheim, California, which sponsors a telephone Hotline for drug addicts and other social problems. He was one of the pastors who pioneered in work with drug addicts in California.

"Ralph wants you to come back Sunday night, to share your testimony then," I was told.

It was exciting. All week long, the announcement was made that I would be present at the Sunday evening session. It was a little frightening, for I felt I was not good at words. All I knew to do was to let out what was in my heart...to let the love of Jesus just spill out. I really had a burden on my heart for the lost and misguided, and I just wanted to share His love and forgiveness with everyone in sight. It was the start of a continuing pattern. I still love to speak of the Lord and His saving grace at every opportunity, to one person or one thousand.

Although some of my problems had been solved, there was still the continuing dilemma of how I could reclaim my daughter, and it was only through constant prayer that I was able to continue being patient in a situation that was a ceaseless worry. Living at home was, for me, no good, for I would see my own child in a setting that I felt was not the best. It was difficult for me to project myself as Shemyiah's mother, with my own mother having the legal right to assume that role. And it was heart-rending to me to feel that my own daughter was headed in the same wrong direction I had taken myself.

I felt the child should have some special guidance, for what child knows what is best for him or her? Yet, whenever I tried to impose any discipline, I'd be stopped in my tracks.

"You're mean!" became familiar words. "Poor baby!" And my daughter would be allowed to pursue the folly of her ways, looking at me as though I were an outsider who had no place in that home.

Unfortunately, there were occasional screaming matches, too — the kind I'd experienced in my own growing up years. There were times when I'd be ready to climb the walls, and only by resorting to the solace of prayer could I cope with the problems. Not helpful were the comments of others around me. "It's too late already," I'd hear. "After a kid is two years old, it's too late!"

And I'd think, "What chance do I have? I can never discipline her. I can never see that she grows up in the right way!" It was another time of total confusion. I'd come to the Lord, and I'd enjoyed a glorious experience that still continued. Yet I was being deprived of bringing up my own child in the way she should go. It was, in a word, a bummer.

All I could do was pray, and my prayers were constant. Though I felt Sheymiah was lost, I did not give up hope. Surely, I thought, the Lord will deliver me — and her — from this tribulation.

Among the problems was a defect in my daughter's little legs. Because of a condition she had been born with, her legs were crooked, and a specialist prescribed corrective shoes with a bar across them, to be worn whenever she took a nap or when she slept at night. She would cry and cry because of the strain this put on her tiny limbs. Yet, it seemed the only thing to do.

Even more complicated was the necessity for proper diet, to help strengthen the legs. The problem was that my mom wouldn't stick to the diet. I'd try to keep her on it, but there would be candy and other snack-type foods slipped to her all too often — the very things she shouldn't have had. When I'd protest, I'd hear the same old words, over and over: "Well, that's what you had when you were little!" I could have noted that the junk didn't do me any good, either, but it wouldn't have helped, so I didn't.

Once again, it seemed to be time to listen to the wise counsel of my brother, Paul. "Why don't you bring Shemyiah to the meeting at the church?" he urged. "Rick Davis is going to be there, and he's blessed with the gift of healing! Maybe..." He left the rest of the sentence unspoken, but I knew what he meant. If it was God's will, perhaps my baby, like many others, could be cured through the healing hand of faith.

When the call came for those needing the healing of God, I wanted to take Shemyiah, but Mom was having no part of that. Although I could see that she was extremely frightened, she insisted on taking the baby herself; I let her go. The main thing was to let God's bidding prevail.

And when the Reverend Rick Davis laid hands on my baby and asked the Lord to send His healing grace to straighten those crooked legs, the Lord answered our prayers with a miracle. Shemyiah's legs took normal shape, then and there, straightening out before our very eyes, and she hasn't had a moment's trouble since!

With the proof of God's wonders in hand with Shemyiah, I thought of my own physical problems, and I hoped that here, too, a miracle could bring about unbelievable change. So I didn't hesitate to bring it up to the Reverend George, after a few days went by.

"I have a backache an awful lot of the time," I said. "I wonder..."

"Maybe one leg is shorter than the other," he interrupted. "I've noticed you have a slight limp sometimes."

"Yes," I confirmed. "Do you think..."

"I don't think — I know!" George said confidently. "I know that God can perform miracles, that He uses us to do them, but that only through Him can they be done."

I nodded. "Praise God!" I murmured, not sure whether I'd been right to mention it to my pastor.

"Why don't you just sit down here and stretch out your legs," George said then. "Let's take a look."

There were several of the congregation members with us, and there were confident nods among them. I sat down and stretched out my legs. You could actually see it — my left leg was shorter than the right, probably as with Shemyiah, a condition existing since I had been born.

Then when George and the others put their hands on my legs and began to pray, I could actually feel a miracle happening! It was like feeling a ripple in my left leg, and when I stood up and walked moments later, my steps were firm and even. My short-ened leg had gained the added length it needed. It has been completely normal ever since, with no more of that aching back I'd learned to accept over the years. Praise God!

Witnessing for the Lord, I learned, was the most rewarding experience I could have, and I seized every opportunity to do so. Like the time when I was driving to church in the rain, and I passed a guy standing by the side of the road, hitchhiking. Perhaps it was because I'd been in that same position myself so many times, but somehow, I heard the voice of the Lord telling me to turn around and go back. So I did.

Gratefully, he got into the car, and I didn't waste any time. "You know, Jesus loves you!" I said. "You want to go to church with me tonight?"

He hesitated, looking at me carefully, so I put on some more pressure. "Oh, come on!" I said. "How about it?"

He gave a shake of his head, as if trying to make sure he'd heard right. Then, confirming the uncertainty, "Huh?"

"Come on!" I pressed him.

"Well, all right."

My new friend not only went to church with me that night, he made a decision for Christ. He's still very much with the Lord today!

That's how it was. I began taking some classes at Mt. San Antonia College — math, English, music — but mostly I was witnessing to those around me, especially the radicals on the campus.

All I could think of was the many people needing Jesus, so I lasted only one semester at the school. But the results were fruitful, just the same. My witnessing led a number of people to the Lord. The Lord would just tell me to do something and I'd do it.

I was walking to my first class one day, for example, and I saw a girl nearby. She just seemed to stand out. I could hear the Lord saying to me, "Go on up to her!" So I did.

"Hey, you know something?" I said. "Jesus loves you so much!"

I went on and shared with her all the things He had done in my life. Before I knew it, she was praying with me, and another lost soul had found the Lord!

I went on to class, rejoicing in what had happened, and when it was over, I hurried outside so I could pass out a supply of religious tracts I'd brought. I was walking along, and once again I heard God's voice.

"Go up to that guy and tell him I love him." So I walked up to a nearby student. I said, "Wait — just a minute! I've got to tell you something!"

The fellow turned toward me, a puzzled look on his face, "God told me to come up to you and tell you He loves you!" I said, handing him one of the tracts. And before he could say anything, I began telling him how I'd come to the Lord and what He had done to change my life around. I wasn't surprised at all when he, too, accepted the Lord.

Another class, another break afterwards, and a repetition of the very same thing — another young man made his decision for Jesus Christ.

I went home, my heart exultant with the events of the memorable day. I was exhausted, both mentally and physically, but when I learned that Mom was going to the store, I heard the Lord tell me, "I want you to go instead."

So I got in Mom's car, and I saw a guy hitchhiking. Again the voice of God in my ear: "Pick him up!" I did, and I immediately began sharing with him about Jesus.

"You know," he broke in finally, "I've been trying to accept the Lord, but I just don't know how. I've been to a lot of churches, and everything, but I just don't know how to do it."

I didn't hesitate. I pulled the car over to the curb and began praying with that young man, and he was no longer in the dark. His decision for Christ, like the others I'd spoken to that wonderful day, was total and sincere. The Lord works in wondrous ways.

Once God told me to go to a doctor's office with a girl friend, and while we were waiting in the office, God told me to share my testimony with everyone there. "You know what?" I announced for all to hear. "Jesus has really changed my life!" I was simply bubbling over with happiness. "He can change yours, too!"

The doctor's office was in a clinic, and quite a few people were waiting, including one who was easily identifiable as a biker. I was obviously just a little too much for him.

"Hey!" he said to me after my initial announcement. "What are you on?"

"Hey, I'm telling you!" I responded. "It's Jesus!"

He got the picture, at least part of it. "How about it?" he asked me. "Are there bikes in heaven?"

I smiled at him, to let him know God's love extends to all His children, regardless of their personal pursuits. "Sure," I said. "Choppers for you in heaven!"

There wasn't time to follow it up, but I hope I had planted a seed of faith in that biker's heart.

While all of this was happening, I kept praying that my problems of regaining custody of my daughter would be solved, and it was evident that the social workers were aware of what was taking place. So at one point, I thought there would be a real possibility. I heard about a so-called Christian House, where I could live and care for my daughter. I received permission from a social worker to take her on a trial basis.

We stayed there for some time, but I found that I could not fit in with the others well. So it was back home for another extended stay, and with a lot of disillusion in my heart. I'd hoped to make a go of it on my own, and here I was back at Mom's again.

I later quietly asked for custody again, meantime having obtained my final divorce from Charles (Erutan) Sipe. Regardless of the fact that my daughter might be lost — as so many told me she would be, since I was not her main guiding influence during her first two years — I felt I could still, with the Lord's help, bring her up in the way she should go.

Afterward I learned that the social workers had called the Reverend George Crites, to get his evaluation of my personal progress. I'd been completely open with them, telling them about my new-found life in the Lord, but they sensibly decided to check it out with other responsible persons.

"She's doing really well," George told them. "Onjya has strong mother instincts, and I think it will be good for both her and the child for her to receive custody. Her life has completely straightened out. You can be sure of it."

God bless my friend and pastor, George Crites! There was a court hearing, but I didn't have to go. Yet even when I had received official custody of my daughter, the only way I could get her away from my mother was to sneak her away from the house, as I'd done so many months before when my husband and I had made our first venture into the haunts of the Manson Family!

What more is there to say? I could cite my late aunt's acceptance of the Lord, not long before she died from cancer. Or I could point to my own father, who made his decision for Christ before his heart gave out. My mother, too, has drawn closer to the Lord. And there have been countless others — yet, I feel ashamed that I have done so little to bring others to Christ! I just want to give of myself more...and more...and more...in His service!

And what about the remaining members of the Manson Family? Several of them — including Charles Manson and others who were on trial when I first met the Family — were convicted of murder and were sentenced to death, with that sentence later changed to life imprisonment when the California State Supreme Court abolished the death penalty. They are much in my prayers.

I understand that both Susan Atkins and Charles "Tex" Watson (both convicted of murder) and perhaps others have given their hearts to God, while some — like Squeaky Fromme and Sandy Good — continue to follow the false philosophy of Satan, as mouthed by Charles Manson. There is yet hope; I shall continue to pray for them all.

What about you? Have you given your heart to Jesus? If not, there's no better time than right now! As you'll read in John 8:12, Jesus said, "I am the light of the world: he that followeth me shall not walk in darkness, but shall have the light of life."

All you have to do is confess with your mouth and believe in your heart that Jesus Christ was resurrected from the dead, and you'll be a new person in the Lord!

For what He has done for me...for what He can do for you...
Praise God!

19

Answers —
It Is Written ...

The Holy Scriptures contain, without a doubt, the most fruitful words ever recorded. No matter what problems you face in life, you'll find an answer in the Bible, if you know where to look — and even if you don't. It will be revealed to you, through the grace of God. "Study to shew thyself approved unto God, a workman that needeth not to be ashamed, rightly dividing the word of truth" (II Timothy 2:15).

There is a scriptural answer to every difficulty, and it is my hope that a brief review of the misled steps I took and some of the Biblical references that point up where I went wrong may be helpful to others in redirecting their own steps to avoid the pitfalls surrounding us.

Where did I go wrong? You've already read about it...the times, the places, the events. Now, let's examine the Holy Word.

Parents — Guide Your Child

"Honour thy father and thy mother: that thy days may be long upon the land which the Lord thy God giveth thee" (Exodus 20:12). The fifth of the Ten Commandments is basic to the association of parent with child, but there are responsibilities on both sides.

As a child, I was willful, stubborn, and not really disciplined as I might have been. The result was a thoroughly distorted life, without proper direction, until the Lord turned it around. While we cannot, of course, reverse that which has gone before, we can look to the present — and to the future — and let God guide our steps accordingly. "Children, obey your parents in the Lord: for this is right. Honour thy father and mother; which is the first commandment with promise; That it may be well with thee, and thou mayest live long on the earth. And, ye fathers, provoke not your children to wrath: but bring them up in the nurture and admonition of the Lord" (Ephesians 6:1-5).

A child cannot be expected to know what is right for him; he must have guidance, and guidance with the hand of God in the background is the best kind, no question. "Foolishness is bound in the heart of a child; but the rod of correction shall drive it far from him" (Proverbs 22:15).

Sometimes I think the Lord's Word was written about me, when I read it and look back to my childhood. "The rod and reproof give wisdom: but a child left to himself bringeth his mother to shame" (Proverbs 29:15). Far too often, in addition to being ignored by my father, handwringing and shouting were the only disciplinary actions taken against me. The result, as detailed in the pages before these, speaks for itself.

Again, "A fool despiseth his father's instruction: but he that regardeth reproof is prudent" (Proverbs 15:5). Need I say more? What reproof I did receive was summarily rejected. I didn't want to listen. And while we're noting foolishness, there's another verse that also applies: "A wise son maketh a glad father: but a foolish son is the heaviness of his mother" (Proverbs 10:1). Obviously, the word "son" applies equally to daughters. And neither has any monopoly on childish foolishness.

"Even a child," according to Proverbs 20:11, "is known by his doings, whether his work be pure, and whether it be right." And since all of us inevitably grow up — for good or for bad — we all need to think seriously on the words of Paul: "When I was a child, I spake as a child, I understood as a child, I thought as a child: but when I became a man, I put away childish things" (I Corinthians 13:11). If we will let Him, the Lord will tell us when the time to put away childish things has come.

Training, Discipline, Obedience Needed

Meantime, "Train up a child in the way he should go: and when he is old, he will not depart from it" (Proverbs 22:6).

How does one go about training up a child in the way he should go? "And, ye fathers, provoke not your children to wrath: but bring them up in the nurture and admonition of the Lord" (Ephesians 6:4).

As I have repeatedly said, I have no wish to condemn my own parents for what I became. Yet, had there been the security of Christian love in that home, might not the results have been different?

Contention between parent and child — and looking back I can see nothing *but* such contention in my own case — is of course one of the problems that must be faced. And contention is cited in the Holy Word more than once: "Only by pride cometh contention: but with the well advised is wisdom" (Proverbs 13:10). "A brother [son] offended is harder to be won than a strong city: and their contentions are like the bars of a castle" (Proverbs 18:19). Yet, contention must be dealt with. "Chasten thy son while there is hope, and let not thy soul spare for his crying" (Proverbs 19:18). Even further: "Withhold not correction from the child: for if thou beatest him with the rod, he shall not die" (Proverbs 23:13).

There are times, of course, when God's Word must not be taken too literally. Studies of modern psychology have proved that "beating with a rod" could be wrongly interpreted, resulting in a far worse situation with respect to parent-child relationships. As in other scriptural references, the "rod" must be given a rather general meaning. "He that spareth his rod hateth his son: but he that loveth him chasteneth him betimes" (Proverbs 13:24).

In a word, discipline is required. "He openeth also their ear to discipline, and commandeth that they return from iniquity" (Job 36:10). Had my own ear been opened to more discipline, the outcome might have been different. Who can say? Guidance, too, must share the way. "Thou shalt guide me with thy counsel, and afterward receive me to glory" (Psalm 73:24).

To an extent, it all comes down to obedience of the parents by the children. When there is discipline and guidance, obedience follows naturally. "Children, obey your parents in the Lord: for this is right" (Ephesians 6:1). And, "Children, obey your parents in all things: for this is well pleasing unto the Lord" (Colossians 3:20).

Examples to Follow

As evidenced by my own actions in following the example of those around me — Janice, Jennie, Chuck, the "Manson Family" — patterns of behavior can be tremendously influential, whether they be good or bad. "For as by one man's disobedience many were made sinners, so by the obedience of one shall many be made righteous" (Romans 5:19). The shining model here, of course, is Jesus Christ Himself: "Though he were a Son, yet learned he obedience by the things which he suffered; And being made perfect, he became the author of eternal salvation unto all them that obey him" (Hebrews 5:8,9). Heed the promise of the Lord: "If they obey and serve him, they shall spend their days in prosperity, and their years in pleasures" (Job 36:11).

My own rebellion against my parents, and my stubbornness in pursuing the paths of evil even though I encountered disastrous results — as when I spent considerable time on two separate occasions in juvenile hall — is pinpointed in the Scriptures: "For rebellion is as the sin of witchcraft, and stubbornness is as iniquity and idolatry" (I Samuel 15:23). If the Holy Bible had been part of my youth, perhaps I would have listened: "My son, keep thy father's commandment, and forsake not the law of thy mother" (Proverbs 6:20).

Trust in the Lord

And if I had but known the Lord in those days as I do now, life would most certainly have been quite different. "Trust in the Lord with all thine heart; and lean not unto thine own understanding. In all thy ways acknowledge him, and he shall direct thy paths" (Proverbs 3:5,6). Similarly, "Thy word is a lamp unto my feet, and a light unto my path" (Psalm 119:105).

Looking backward, it seems much of my early life was spent in anger. It would have been better, otherwise. "Let all bitterness, and wrath, and anger, and clamour, and evil speaking, be put away from you, with all malice: And be ye kind one to another, tenderhearted, forgiving one another, even as God for Christ's

sake hath forgiven you" (Ephesians 4:31,32). Speaking of anger,
"Be not hasty in thy spirit to be angry: for anger resteth in the
bosom of fools" (Ecclesiastes 7:9). But there's another side to
anger, also: "Fathers, provoke not your children to anger, lest
they be discouraged" (Colossians 3:21). Reasoning, not anger, is
the key to accomplishment.

Perhaps the real essential of the relationship between the
Scriptures and the rearing of children, as well as an enduring guide
to successful living is contained in II Timothy 3:16,17: "All
scripture is given by inspiration of God, and is profitable for
doctrine, for reproof, for instruction in righteousness: That the
man of God may be perfect, thoroughly furnished unto all good
works."

Among the many mistakes of my youth was the belief that
outward appearance was all-important. The result, of course, was
neglect of the inner person, and the outcome was predictable.
You'll find it in God's Word: "Whose adorning let it not be that
outward adorning of plaiting the hair, and of wearing of gold, or of
putting on of apparel; But let it be the hidden man of the heart, in
that which is not corruptible, even the ornament of a meek and
quiet spirit, which is in the sight of God of great price" (I Peter
3:3,4).

Hope for the Sinful

As you have read in these pages, much of the sin that exists in
this world existed in my life, at one time or another. It is only in the
hope that the salvation of the Lord may reach others, as it did me,
that I have set down the sordid record that is mine. It's detailed in
the Scriptures, too: "Now the works of the flesh are manifest,
which are these; Adultery, fornication uncleanness, lascivious-
ness, Idolatry, witchcraft, hatred, variance, emulations, wrath,
strife, seditions, heresies, Envyings, murders, drunkenness,
revellings, and such like: of the which I tell you before, as I have
also told you in time past, that they which do such things shall not
inherit the kingdom of God" (Galatians 5:19-21).

But there is always hope. I was not aware of it, of course, but
"There hath no temptation taken you but such as is common to
man: but God is faithful, who will not suffer you to be tempted

above that ye are able; but will with the temptation also make a way to escape, that ye may be able to bear it" (I Corinthians 10:13). Again, had I but known, "He that covereth his sins shall not prosper: but whoso confesseth and forsaketh them shall have mercy" (Proverbs 28:13). And if I had known the Scriptures and been able to apply them to my life at an earlier time, "Be not overcome of evil, but overcome evil with good" (Romans 12:21).

Had I but known it, "Treasures of wickedness profit nothing; but righteousness delivereth from death" (Proverbs 10:2). Everyone should be fully aware that the Lord sees all, knows all: "O God, thou knowest my foolishness; and my sins are not hid from thee" (Psalm 69:5).

My parents might well have said, as did the Lord: "Yet I had planted thee a noble vine, wholly a right seed: how then art thou turned into the degenerate plant of a strange vine unto me?" (Jeremiah 2:21).

Learn from My Errors

How, indeed, can others learn from my errors? Again look to the Bible. I might well have taken note, on that first trip with Janice to West Covina, that "Wine is a mocker, strong drink is raging: and whosoever is deceived thereby is not wise" (Proverbs 20:1). Or, certainly after the first time I was busted for being drunk and disorderly, I should have learned from my mistakes. Had I known the Scriptures, I could have said, with Paul: "Let us walk honestly, as in the day; not in rioting and drunkenness, not in chambering and wantonness, not in strife and envying" (Romans 13:13). I could also have heeded his later words: "And be not drunk with wine, wherein is excess; but be filled with the Spirit" (Ephesians 5:18).

There was the incident at the store, when I was busted for swiping the eye make-up. No question about it, I knew this was wrong. I didn't even have to have the direct knowledge that an admonition was included in the Ten Commandments: "Thou shalt not steal" (Exodus 20:15).

And there were the later times when, despite bitter experience in a physical sense, I did not hesitate to succumb to the lusts of the flesh: "Let not sin therefore reign in your mortal body, that ye should obey it in the lusts thereof" (Romans 6:12). Although I realize now that the Lord had a purpose for me, I could wish that I had had opportunity to heed His directions: "Flee also youthful lusts: but follow righteousness, faith, charity, peace, with them that call on the Lord out of a pure heart" (II Timothy 2:22).

When Life Seems Hopeless

There came times in my life when I felt it was useless to go on; there was nothing to live for. True, when it happened the first time, at Mouse's apartment, I was high on acid and speed, while at later times I could use no such excuse. The Bible cites this situation, as it does most others: "Even in laughter the heart is sorrowful; and the end of that mirth is heaviness" (Proverbs 14:13). Job, of course, is the epitome of the dejection that leads to suicidal tendencies: "My soul is weary of my life; I will leave my complaint upon myself; I will speak in the bitterness of my soul" (Job 10:1).

Yet, there is always hope. All we have to do is turn to Him in our depression or desperation. "Be strong and of a good courage, fear not, nor be afraid of them: for the Lord thy God, he it is that doth go with thee; he will not fail thee, nor forsake thee" (Deuteronomy 31:6). Put another way, "What shall we then say to these things? If God be for us, who can be against us?" (Romans 8:31).

When we departed Joshua Tree in a panic because of the rumored earthquake, none of us, I'm sure, considered the possibility that our headlong flight had been anticipated and made unnecessary many centuries ago. "God is our refuge and strength, a very present help in trouble. Therefore will not we fear, though the earth be removed, and though the mountains be carried into the midst of the sea" (Psalm 46:1,2).

It was basic insecurity, of course, that sent us packing on that occasion as well as many others. Should insecurity be your lot, take heart. "For I the Lord thy God will hold thy right hand, saying unto thee, Fear not; I will help thee" (Isaiah 41:13). It's only true. "The Lord is my light and my salvation; whom shall I fear? the Lord is the strength of my life; of whom shall I be afraid?" (Psalm 27:1).

Beware False Prophets

Why was I willing to accept the Charles Manson philosophy as

truth? Why did I even wonder whether Manson's claim to be Jesus
Christ had any validity? It's there in the Word; I am not the only
one to have been taken in over the years. "For many shall come in
my name, saying, I am Christ; and shall deceive many" (Matthew
24:5).

That's only one reference to the situation. There are others:
"And many false prophets shall rise, and shall deceive many"
(Matthew 24:11). "For there shall arise false Christs, and false
prophets, and shall shew great signs and wonders; insomuch that,
if it were possible, they shall deceive the very elect" (Matthew
24:24). For a long time, I followed false prophets and a false
Christ; deceived, I was — but no more, for the reality that is Jesus
Christ is now part of my life.

Because the falsity on which the entire "Manson Family" was
based became so much a part of my life, other Biblical references
to this circumstance are worth noting. "Beloved, believe not every
spirit, but try the spirits whether they are of God: because many
false prophets are going out into the world" (I John 4:1). And
again, "But there were false prophets also among the people, even
as there shall be false teachers among you, who privily shall bring
in damnable heresies, even denying the Lord that bought them and
bring upon themselves swift destruction. Any many shall follow
their pernicious ways; by reason of whom the way of truth shall be
evil spoken of. And through covetousness shall they with feigned
words make merchandise of you: whose judgment now of a long
time lingereth not, and their damnation slumbereth not" (II Peter
2:1-3). Can anyone doubt the Bible's foretelling of events of our
day? It happened!

And yet one more reference: "Beware of false phophets, which
come to you in sheep's clothing, but inwardly they are ravening
wolves" (Matthew 7:15). The description fits perfectly, as does
this further word in II Peter 2:10: "But chiefly them that walk after
the flesh in the lust of uncleanness, and despise government. Pre-
sumptuous are they, selfwilled, they are not afraid to speak evil of
dignities."

I've mentioned that Charles Manson thought of the English
singing group, the Beatles, as the four angels of Revelation, and
of course the "bottomless pit" presumed to be hidden away in
Death Valley was very much a part of the distorted Manson pro-

nouncements. It's covered in Revelation 9:1, even to the extent
of Manson's proclaiming himself as the "fifth angel": "And the fifth
angel sounded, and I saw a star fall from heaven unto the earth:
and to him was given the key of the bottomless pit." Talk about
false prophets! I'm sure no more clear example could be found
anywhere!

Confessing Our Sins

When the time came in my life when I could no longer hide my
sin (of smoking) and the Lord told me I had to do something about
it, I could have taken my direction straight from the Bible. "Confess your faults one to another, and pray one for another, that ye
may be healed. The effectual fervent prayer of a righteous man
availeth much" (James 5:16). Amen! "If we confess our sins, he is
faithful and just to forgive us our sins, and to cleanse us from all
unrighteousness" (I John 1:9).

Speaking of sins, there's one more reference that covers a lot of
the world's problems: "But now ye also put off all these; anger,
wrath, malice, blasphemy, filthy communication out of your
mouth. Lie not one to another, seeing that ye have put off the old
man with his deeds; And have put on the new man, which is
renewed in knowledge afer the image of him that created him"
(Colossians 3:8-10).

It's only truth. It's the same truth I was constantly searching for
throughout my life, truth that I found only when Jesus Christ came
into my life. Had I but known, I could have found truth far sooner,
and it is my fervent prayer that you will use my mistakes to avoid
them for yourself. Truth? It's evident throughout the pages of the
Good Book.

Know the Truth

"And ye shall know the truth, and the truth shall make you free"
(John 8:32). "Jesus saith unto him, I am the way, the truth, and
the life: no man cometh unto the Father, but by me" (John 14:6).
"Sanctify them through thy truth: thy word is truth" (John 17:17).

All of the above verses are from the New Testament, of course.
But truth stood up in the words of the ancient prophets, too. "For

the Lord is good; his mercy is everlasting; and his truth endureth of all generations" (Psalm 100:5). "That I might make thee know the certainty of the words of truth; that thou mightest answer the words of truth to them that send unto thee?" (Proverbs 22:21).

The spirit of truth is evident in the Word of God...a spirit that must dwell within each of us. "He that hath no rule over his own spirit is like a city that is broken down, and without walls" (Proverbs 25:28). I'm grateful to the Lord that the result of a twisted life has become one in which I do now have rule over my own spirit, the spirit of truth.

Hope for Everyone

Much of what I have enumerated here from the Word has been in reference to the troubles I encountered. But there is a much more positive side, too, that I believe bears mentioning, for there is hope for everyone in the Scriptures. "Grace and peace be multiplied unto you through the knowledge of God, and of Jesus our Lord.

"According as his divine power hath given unto us all things that pertain unto life and godliness, through the knowledge of him that hath called us to glory and virtue:

"Whereby are given unto us exceeding great and precious promises: that by these ye might be partakers of the divine nature, having escaped the corruption that is in the world through lust.

"And beside this, giving all diligence, add to your faith, virtue; and to virtue, knowledge;

"And to knowledge, temperance; and to temperance, patience; and to patience, godliness;

"And to godliness, brotherly kindness; and to brotherly kindness, charity.

"For if these things be in you, and abound, they make you that ye shall neither be barren nor unfruitful in the knowledge of our Lord Jesus Christ.

"But he that lacketh these things is blind, and cannot see afar off, and hath forgotten that he was purged from his old sins.

"Wherefore the rather, brethren, give diligence to make your calling and election sure: for if ye do these things, ye shall never fall" (II Peter 1:3-10).

One of the most difficult of all virtues, at least in my own attempts to achieve them, is patience. Many of us, I believe, are by our very nature impatient.   Yet, patience is all-important: "Knowing this, that the trying of your faith worketh patience. But let patience have her perfect work, that ye may be perfect and entire, wanting nothing" (James 1:3-4).

Again looking backward, to the rebellious times of my youth, I have to wonder what might have transpired under differing circumstances. There are admonitions that I believe can help others take a different way. "A soft answer turneth away wrath: but grievous words stir up anger" (Proverbs 15:1).

Love — the Greatest of All

Love, of course, provides many of the answers to our problems — love of the Lord, love in a spiritual sense. "For God so loved the world, that he gave his only begotten Son, that whosoever believeth in him should not perish, but have everlasting life" (John 3:16).

As for those around us, the Word again gives us guidance: "Be kindly affectioned one to another with brotherly love; in honour preferring one another" (Romans 12:10). It would be easy for me to have hate in my heart for those who misled me throughout my life, but I thank God there is none. Instead, I pray for those who misused me, according to his Word: "But I say unto you, Love your enemies, bless them that curse you, do good to them that hate you, and pray for them which despitefully use you, and persecute you" (Matthew 5:44).

Nor could I ever condemn others for what I was. "Therefore thou are inexcusable, O man, whosoever thou art that judgest; for wherein thou judgest another, thou condemnest thyself; for thou that judgest doest the same things" (Romans 2:1).

Trust in God

As I see it, the answer to all our problems lies in trust in God. Again, you'll find it in His Holy Word: "Be strong and of a good courage, fear not, nor be afraid of them: for the Lord thy God, he it is that doth go with thee; he will not fail thee, nor forsake thee"

(Deuteronomy 31:6). "Submit yourselves therefore to God. Resist the devil, and he will flee from you" (James 4:7). How I wish I'd known *that* somewhere along the way!

Peace of mind can be yours; only believe! "Peace I leave with you, my peace I give unto you: not as the world giveth, give I unto you. Let not your heart be troubled, neither let it be afraid" (John 14:27). You can get more from life, following His Word: "Thou wilt shew me the path of life: in thy presence is fulness of joy; at thy right hand there are pleasures for evermore" (Psalm 16:11).

How can you achieve the satisfaction of God's presence? "Ask, and it shall be given you; seek, and ye shall find; knock, and it shall be opened unto you: For every one that asketh receiveth; and he that seeketh findeth; and to him that knocketh it shall be opened" (Matthew 7:7,8).

Salvation can be yours, as it is mine. Only believe! "For the grace of God that bringeth salvation hath appeared to all men.

"Teaching us that, denying ungodliness and worldly lusts, we should live soberly, righteously, and godly, in this present world;

"Looking for that blessed hope, and the glorious appearing of the great God and our Saviour Jesus Christ;

"Who gave himself for us, that he might redeem us from all iniquity, and purify unto himself a peculiar people, zealous of good works.

"These things speak, and exhort, and rebuke with all authority. Let no man despise thee" (Titus 2:11-15).

Let the Holy Spirit In

You will recall that one of the most joyous times of my life came when I was baptized in the Holy Spirit. "I indeed baptize you with water unto repentance; but he that cometh after me is mightier than I, whose shoes I am not worthy to bear: he shall baptize you with the Holy Ghost, and with fire" (Matthew 3:11).

And the Holy Spirit becomes an all-important part of our lives, for what He brings to us: "But the fruit of the Spirit is love, joy, peace, longsuffering, gentleness, goodness, faith, Meekness, temperance: against such there is no law" (Galatians 5:22,23).

You, too, can spead the gospel. "Let your light so shine before men, that they may see your good works, and glorify your Father which is in heaven" (Matthew 5:16).

Just keep this prayer ever in mind: "Let the words of my mouth, and the meditation of my heart, be acceptable in thy sight, O Lord, my strength, and my redeemer" (Psalm 19:14).

If I have been able to touch one heart in the pages of this book, all glory be to God. If that heart is yours, praise God! To every reader, I can find no better words to wish you well than these, which you'll find in Jude 24-25:

"Now unto him that is able to keep you from falling, and to present you faultless before the presence of his glory with exceeding joy,

"To the only wise God our Saviour, be glory and majesty, dominion and power, both now and ever. Amen."